HONORARY TIGER

HONORARY TIGER
THE LIFE OF BILLY ARJAN SINGH

DUFF HART-DAVIS

Methuen

Published by Methuen 2005

10 9 8 7 6 5 4 3 2 1

© Duff Hart-Davis, 2005

Duff Hart-Davis has asserted his right under
the Copyright, Designs and Patents Act, 1988
to be identified as the author of this work

First published in 2005 in India by
The Lotus Collection, an imprint of
Roli Books Pvt. Ltd.
M-75, G.K. II Market, New Delhi 110 048

First published in the United Kingdon
in 2005 by Methuen Publishing Limited,
11–12 Buckingham Gate
London SW1E 6LB

ISBN: 0 413 77553 4

Printed and bound in Great Britain by
St. Edmundsbury Press, Bury St. Edmunds, Suffolk

CONTENTS

ACKNOWLEDGEMENTS

M y principal debt is to Billy himself, who answered questions with exemplary patience, and shared his great knowledge of Indian wildlife with the utmost generosity. His sister Amar Commander, equally patient, contributed many amusing anecdotes about family life. I am hugely indebted, also, to his sister-in-law Mira, whose exceptional skill as a hostess has made Tiger Haven a wonderfully comfortable place to stay. It is very sad that her husband Balram – Billy's younger brother – did not live to see this book published.

I am particularly grateful to the following for their help:

Amanda Aspinall, Lady Sally Aspinall, Simon Bazeley, Rahul Brijnath, Lisa Choegyal, Priya Commander, Simon Commander, Ashish Chandola, Jim Edwards, Aqeel Farooqi, Sarah Giles, K.K. Gurung, Arabella Heathcote-Amory, Sunil Jaiswal, Dilip Khatau, Chuck McDougal, Tom Maschler, Nicky Marx, Johnny Moorehead, Hari Singh Nat, James Osborne, Lucy Peck, Mary Plage, Bittu Sahgal, George Schaller, Toby Sinclair, (late) Mahindar Singh, Mukuljit Singh, Xenia Singh, Haik Sookias, Valmik Thapar, John Wakefield, Colin Willock, Belinda Wright.

FOREWORD

This is the story of a man who has devoted nearly fifty years of his life to the welfare of India's big cats. Billy Arjan Singh's fame as a champion of tigers and leopards has travelled far beyond his native shores: he is known as a latter-day version of the legendary hunter-naturalist Jim Corbett. But I suspect that many people who have read his books imagine him to be rather dour. Always, it seems, he has been at loggerheads with corrupt and inefficient forest officers, always seeking to defend the tiger and the leopard against the ever-increasing pressures of human population. His sheer commitment may make him appear arrogant, argumentative and excessively serious.

In fact he is none of these. There is no doubt that he cares passionately about animals, and he is as fearless in standing up to human opponents as he is in walking the jungle armed only with a stick. Yet that is only what one might call his professional persona – and in some ways his behaviour is uncannily like that of a big male tiger. He has often said that the jungle animals seem to treat him as a kind of honorary tiger – and that is what, over the years, he has become.

Out in the forest he has ceaselessly patrolled his chosen range, repelling human intruders with explosive roars; but at home he is a gentler being altogether: just as a male tiger chivalrously allows his own cubs to feed with him on a kill, so among his family and friends Billy is modest, self-effacing and endowed with almost childlike charm. He treats women with old-fashioned courtliness, inspires fierce, lifelong loyalty in his associates, and has a strong, rather mischievous sense of humour.

Once when staying with him I stumbled against a small table in the sitting room, provoking the immediate taunt, 'Anything else you'd like to kick over?' Another time, I was stricken by a severe stomach upset, and spent most of the night in and out of the bathroom, so that, come first light, I was in no shape to go out for my customary jog in the jungle. I certainly did not feel like meeting the big tiger who was master of the range immediately behind the house.

At about 6 a.m. Billy began his normal routine of weight-lifting, clanking away on the flat roof above the terrace while the air was still relatively cool and the dense overnight mist was beginning to thin. During a break he came to tap on my window and said accusingly, 'Duff, you idle beggar. Why aren't you running?'

'I've been poisoned by something I ate,' I told him.

'Oh, God!'

'I'm on the mend, though. I'll join you later for a cup of tea.'

So at seven I hauled myself up, got dressed and crept outside into the low-slanted early sunlight. At once Billy started up again.

'You ought to be running by now,' he teased me.

'I know,' I agreed. 'But I didn't feel I could cope with the big tiger when I was in that state.'

Whereupon he crooned in his jungly voice, 'No – but you could have shat in his face and run like hell.'

That was Billy all over. When not exasperated by the futility and venality of Indian bureaucrats, he is full of such nipping jokes – but it is the animals and their fate that obsess him, and it is to the wild creatures of India that he has given the best years of his life.

Gloucestershire,   DUFF HART-DAVIS
January 2005

ONE

DEATH IN THE JUNGLE

On the evening of 12 January 1980 a labourer who had been working on the road through the Dudhwa National Park, on India's border with Nepal, failed to return to the park headquarters. By the time a search party set out into the forest on elephants, darkness had fallen, but although the rescuers claimed to have seen two tigers mating near the spot where they thought the man should be, and fired off a volley of shots, they found no trace of him. They were convinced that he had been killed by a tiger – and sure enough, when they returned in a jeep next evening, they spotted his body lying in the undergrowth beneath the tall, straight trunks of the sal hardwood trees. Yet it was not until the third day that they recovered the corpse – and then they found that only the genitals had been eaten.

On that third day the park authorities sought the help of Billy Arjan Singh, who lived (and still lives) at Tiger Haven, the house he built on the edge of the forest two miles west of the park headquarters. A short, sturdy man, then sixty-two, with an immensely powerful physique built up by regular weight-lifting, Billy had spent the past twenty years acting as a voluntary wildlife warden, battling to protect the creatures of the reserve. During that time he had established an international reputation as one of India's leading conservationists, and in 1976 he had been presented with the World Wildlife Fund's Gold Medal for saving an important herd of swamp deer – the first Asian to receive the award.

Nobody questioned his dedication to Dudhwa's wildlife, or his expert knowledge of tigers; yet on his home ground he had often been in conflict with officers of the forest department who ran the national park, for their standards of honesty and endeavour by no means matched his own.

The worst cause of friction was a unique experiment which he had initiated nearly four years earlier. In September 1976, with the direct support of the Indian prime minister, Mrs Indira Gandhi, he had brought out a three-month-old female tiger cub from Twycross Zoo in England, with the aim of rearing her in and around his house and releasing her into the jungle. His intention had been to show that it should, in theory, be possible, to re-stock tiger reserves with animals bred in captivity, and his experience with Tara had vindicated him completely: having grown to maturity, loose about his home, the tigress responded to the call of her kind and departed into the jungle, where in due course she mated with a wild tiger and began to produce litters of cubs.

The trouble was that her return to the forest in January 1978 coincided almost exactly with an unprecedented outbreak of maneating in Kheri, the district of Uttar Pradesh in which Billy lives. In fact the root of the problem lay across the border to the north, in Nepal, where such huge tracts of forest had been cleared to create farmland that the resident tigers, deprived of their habitat, had been driven southwards into India, creating a temporary surplus and shortage of prey in and around the Dudhwa National Park.

At the time, however, this was not obvious – and what could not be denied was the fact that two months after Tara had gone wild, tigers began to pick off one human being after another, until terror gripped the villagers, and people began blaming Billy. 'It's your bloody tiger that's doing it,' they said bitterly. 'Because she was brought up with humans, she's not afraid of them, and she's turned maneater.' Billy knew, or at any rate passionately hoped, that this was not true. Several times, when examining the site of a kill, he had found from the pug marks that the villain was a male, so that Tara was immediately exonerated, and of several tigresses shot on suspicion of being maneaters, none had borne any resemblance to Tara, whose unique facial markings he knew by heart.

All the same, by the beginning of 1980 the death toll had risen to over eighty, of which his enemies credited Tara with thirty-odd, and as he drove out to the scene of the kill in January, he was once again full of foreboding. Could she, after all, be the culprit this time?

By the time he reached the site, the immediate area had been so thoroughly trampled that no useful evidence remained; but close at hand he found pug marks which he recognized as those of a tigress known to him as the Median (her name derived from the fact that she had attached herself to the big male on the home range between his liaisons with two other tigresses). Alongside her tracks were those of her single cub, then about eighteen months old and still at heel. Billy concluded that it must have been the Median and her daughter that the rescue party had seen.

Maneaters generally start killing humans because they are injured or handicapped, and cannot any longer catch or subdue their normal prey; but Billy knew from frequent earlier sightings that both these tigresses were in full health. Nevertheless, from that moment the Median was under suspicion, and this intensified in June when another man was taken near the Dudhwa railway station.

Then, at the beginning of August, Billy returned from a trip to London to find that the tigress had killed his own assistant tracker, Lallu. It was a deliberate attack within a few hundred yards of Tiger Haven on the dirt track that leads to the house. Examination of the site showed that she had crouched behind a tree before jumping on the man as he walked past, and sunk her canines into his neck, killing him instantly. Once again she had bitten off the genitals, leaving the rest of the body intact. To Billy, this suggested that she was puzzled by the unfamiliar shape of her victims: a tiger's normal prey such as a deer or a pig is four-footed, and moves with its body in a horizontal posture, whereas humans go around upright. But even if the Median was not yet a confirmed maneater, she was certainly a man-killer – and she had put herself in mortal danger.

Because the latest incident had taken place so close to Tiger Haven, the clamour for Tara's blood grew louder than ever – and no one was more vociferous in condemning the zoo-bred tigress than the park director, R.L. Singh, whose office and headquarters were in Dudhwa, two miles from Billy's home. Tara, he insisted, must be eliminated. Trying in vain to persuade him that the culprit was the Median, Billy pointed out that at least six tigresses were active in the area, and that because accurate identification was almost impossible in the jungle, no effective action could be taken until another incident occurred – otherwise an innocent tiger might be shot, and the killer might survive to strike again. Project Tiger – India's all-out attempt to save the species from extinction –

was in full swing: the tiger had become the national animal, and each and every one was precious.

The next attack came soon enough. On 8 November an old sweeping woman wandered off to relieve herself in the teak plantation outside the perimeter fence of the park headquarters compound, only to be grabbed, killed and dragged down a steep bank into a patch of tall grass. R.L. Singh was then in Lakhimpur, more than two hours' drive away; but instead of going to fetch Billy, who was within easy call, members of the park staff rode out on two elephants to retrieve the body. Had Billy been with them, he would have had a good chance of despatching the tigress there and then, because she was spotted close to the woman's remains. As it was, the animal disappeared, having eaten only one arm and a breast.

For the rest of the day panic reigned in the compound – yet at about 4.30 p.m. a man called Asghar, one of the elephant charkattas, or fodder-cutters, walked down into a ravine to answer a call of nature. He too was seized and carried off – and when his companions went in search of him half an hour later, they found nothing but his spear and water container lying in a pool of blood. This time they did send for Billy; but because darkness had fallen before he reached the scene, he could not follow the line of the drag.

Only in the morning did a search party discover the body, more than half of which had been eaten. Confronted by the grisly evidence, Billy agreed that the tigress must be shot as soon as possible: as he himself said, 'familiarity had bred contempt, and humans were now included in her natural prey species.' R.L. Singh – a smooth-looking man who sported a neatly-trimmed dark beard, perhaps in the hope that it would distract attention from his hair which had turned prematurely grey – hurried back from Lakhimpur, and in a radio message from Lucknow his boss, the chief wildlife warden of U.P., officially declared the animal a maneater.

During the day Billy got his tracker, Jackson, to build a machan, or tree platform, above the spot where Asghar had been killed, and, together with the park director, sat up until 9 p.m. with his .375 magnum rifle over a buffalo tethered as bait. The tigress did not return, but in the morning she came out of the grass and began calling loudly as she moved off to the north-west, parallel to the metalled road that leads through the forest to the Nepal border.

R.L. Singh went after her on an elephant, armed only with a borrowed 12-bore shotgun loaded with buckshot – a weapon dangerously inadequate for the task – and when she came out on to the road, he followed her at a distance for more than a mile. But he also sent a messenger to fetch Billy, who arrived with his big rifle to find that now three tigers were involved: the Median, her nearly full-grown cub, and another sub-adult animal, all of which had disappeared into a stand of six-foot-high grass alongside the road.

That night, to hold the killer in the area, he staked out another bait in the jungle about fifty yards from the road, at a spot where two forest tracks formed a small crossing. In the morning, when he went back to see what had happened, he found that the tigers had duly killed the buffalo, but had not managed to break the tethering rope; so, advancing cautiously with loaded rifle at the ready – for he felt certain the maneater was somewhere very close – he untied the tether and withdrew.

Sometime during the morning the tigers dragged their kill further into the forest, where the straight, dark-brown trunks of sal trees towered above the four-foot-tall undergrowth. The bushes were both thick enough, in patches, to make the killer feel secure, and scattered enough to give a rifleman a good chance of a shot if she moved from one clump to another.

In the afternoon, therefore, an armed party set out in pursuit: one elephant carried Billy, with his .375, Jackson and R.L.Singh, who by then had acquired an ancient .375 with a broken safety catch, hurriedly sent down from Lucknow. The men were perched on a khatola– a padded platform, like an inverted table with very short legs – behind the mahout, or driver, who sat astride the elephant's neck, steering it by digging his big toes into the backs of its ears. On a second elephant were Billy's brother Balram, equipped with the family's .500 double-barrelled express rifle, and three American tourists, who happened to be staying at Tiger Haven and had arrived at a (for them) thrillingly opportune moment. Billy would have preferred them to stay out of the way, but they were immensely excited by the prospect of a hunt, and Balram had persuaded him that he could bring them along.

Billy had handled firearms ever since he was a boy, but he knew that R.L. Singh had never fired a rifle at a live target, and so he had little confidence in his ability as a marksman. All the same, since they were in the park director's territory, he felt constrained to give him first shot.

The hunt proved short and sharp. Following the drag-line through the grass, the elephants moved forward. Hardly had they come on the remains of the kill when a tiger started up out of the undergrowth. R.L. Singh raised his rifle and would have fired, had Billy not grabbed his arm and hissed, 'Wait! This is the cub!' Seconds later another tiger rose out of the bushes and sat staring at the elephant, no more than ten yards off. From her very boldness Billy realized at once that this was the Median, covering the retreat of her cub, and not in the least fazed by the proximity of humans.

'Shoot!' he whispered.

R.L. Singh fired, from point-blank range. Splinters of wood flew from a branch between rifle and target, but the tigress had clearly been hit, for she gave a lurch before bounding away to the right. From all round in the jungle peacocks, startled by the boom of the heavy rifle, let fly their warning calls – *Ay-yorrh! Ay-yorrh!*

Silence fell. Then gradually the monkeys and smaller birds resumed their normal conversations. After waiting a few minutes, Billy told the mahout to make the elephant kneel, and Jackson slid down over its tail to inspect the point of impact. On the ground he found a lump of skin and flesh, indicating that the tiger had been hit somewhere in the gut. How seriously she was wounded, it was impossible to tell – so Jackson climbed back to his perch and both elephants moved forward, starting to sweep through the bushes in ever-widening arcs. ·

After advancing barely a hundred yards to their right, the party spotted the tigress lying on her side, apparently lifeless, with a patch of blood showing that she had been hit low in the stomach. As a precaution Billy told R.L. Singh to put another bullet into her, which he did. When the impact provoked no reaction, Billy got down, threw the empty cartridge-case on to the body, and then, as a final test, tried the old hunter's trick of pulling the tiger's tail.

Everyone could see that the maneater was dead. To Billy she looked about six years old, in prime condition, and bore no physical defect that could have accounted for her fatal predilection.

R.L. Singh's first words were, 'It's Tara, isn't it?'

'No,' said Billy. 'It's nothing like her. It's the Median.' Not only were the facial markings different from Tara's: the biological fact, which everyone except R.L. Singh understood, was that Tara, at just over four, was not old enough to have borne the two-year-old cub which had been the Median's constant companion.

In any event, everyone came down off the elephants and took photographs. When the park director suggested that the best course would be to bury the tigress there and then, in the forest, Billy agreed, and he went off home thinking that the interment was already taking place.

That should have been the end of the saga – but in fact it was only the beginning. Next morning Billy still felt puzzled by the circumstances of the shot, and when he returned to the scene for another look round, he found that an inch-thick branch had been cut off by the director's first bullet, deflecting it into the target. Taking the branch with him, he walked down to the park headquarters and presented it to R.L. Singh, congratulating him on his good fortune.

He was startled to find that, far from burying the tigress's body, the park director had had it taken back to his headquarters and laid out in a trailer, surrounded and neatly covered by fresh grass, so that only its head was showing. As Billy was standing there, Singh set off with the trailer hitched behind his jeep on a triumphal tour of the principal towns in the district, proceeding through nearby Pallia to Lakhimpur, Sitapur and finally Lucknow, the state capital, where the chief wildlife warden of U.P. had his headquarters. Along the way he stopped again and again in villages so that people could come and stare at the ravening monster from which he had heroically freed them.

The further he went, the wilder and more fanciful his stories became. He did not, of course, let on that his first shot had been a prodigious fluke – that if the bullet had not been deflected by striking the branch, it might well have missed altogether; but he described how Billy had stood over the fallen monster with tears coursing down his face, stricken by grief at the death of his former pet.

When the U.P. government, in gratitude, presented R.L. Singh with the head and skin of the tiger, mounted (at a cost of Rs 6,000, or over two years' wages for an average peasant), he installed the stuffed body in his office and posed beside it for photographs, regaling journalists with lurid accounts of how the tiger had charged him before he fearlessly gunned it down.

He corroborated these fantasies in articles of his own, and excelled himself by telling newspaper reporters that Billy had wanted to use Tara for purposes of espionage: he had hoped to fit her with a radio collar so that he could transmit messages to Soviet satellites. Twenty years after the event, he produced *Tara the Cocktail Tigress*, a book whose mendacity was in a class of its own. He could find no way of accounting for the fact that Tara was too young to have had a two-year-old cub, but he sought to explain the discrepancy in markings by claiming that the stripes on a tiger's face change as it grows older. Billy agreed that markings do sometimes alter as a young animal puts on bulk and fills out its frame, but Tara had three unique points of patterning which remained the same throughout her life: one was a set of stripes like an inverted catapult on her left cheek, another an isolated spot above her left eye, and the third a small triangle of black on her left hind leg. Photographs taken long after the death of the Median confirm that she was living wild.

Billy, meanwhile, was left to carry on his one-man battle to preserve Dudhwa's big cats. Naturally, he was upset by the Median's untimely death, for the tigress had been an old acquaintance: he had often seen her in the jungle, and in several close encounters she had had a chance of killing him. Beyond that, he had dedicated the best part of his life to the welfare of tigers, and the last thing he wanted was to see one shot.

At least the right animal had been killed, and a genuine maneater eliminated. At least he had the comfort of knowing that Tara had once again been absolved from blame. But he knew, also, that clashes between people and carnivores were bound to continue, because the Indian population was rocketing out of control: humans desperate for living space were continually encroaching on the tigers' territory, and the two species could not co-exist on the same ground. Further, he knew that the authorities in the forest service – corrupt and incompetent as they were – would declare other tigers maneaters without any thorough investigation, so that many innocent animals would meet their doom. He felt that, already, Project Tiger was proving dismally ineffective, and that it was only a matter of time before the kings and queens of the jungle were driven to extinction.

The most unfortunate result of the row about Tara was the fact that, from the moment of her introduction, he was dogged by the insensate hostility of the Indian tiger establishment. The fact that he had devoted himself to saving the country's wildlife seemed to make no impact on the babus (clerks or bureaucrats) in Lucknow and Delhi: his advice was rarely sought, his ideas for improving the situation were ignored, his private machan was destroyed by employees of the forest service, and attempts were made to prosecute him.

It is hard to escape the impression that jealousy played a major part in this sustained campaign of denigration. The fact was that Billy pressed ahead and did things, while his critics sat on one committee after another and passed anodyne resolutions. Another factor that rankled was his uncompromising honesty: although most officials of the forest service were happy enough to accept bribes, he never would. As that formidable prime minister, Indira Gandhi, pointed out, the efforts of one determined individual on the ground were more beneficial to wildlife than all the waffle of babudom – and the babus knew this, and did not like it.

TWO

BORN KILLER

What is it that turns a mindless killer of animals into a conservationist? Many men lose their blood-lust as they grow older, but scarcely any change as comprehensively as Arjan Singh did: as a boy he gunned down every creature in sight, yet he went on to espouse the cause of wildlife with the utmost fervour. He grew up in an environment where the shooting of leopards and tigers was part of everyday life; but later, guided only by his conscience and the observations he made when he went to live at close quarters with the animals, he metamorphosed into one of the most tenacious champions of wildlife that India has ever produced.

He was born on 15 August 1917 at Gorakhpur, in the United Provinces (now Uttar Pradesh), and although he was christened Arjan, his aunt Amrit at first sight called him 'Bill Bodey' after a man in the news, and he became known by the nickname which has clung to him for life. Scion of a princely Sikh family, he was the son of Kanwar Jasbir Singh, grandson of Raja Sir Harnam Singh, and great grandson of Maharaja Randhir Singh, the ruler of Kapurthala, who lived from 1830 to 1870.

The Kapurthalas were one of the great families of the Punjab. The name of their clan, Ahluwalia (taken – some say – from a little village and meaning, modestly, 'potato'), derived from Jassa Singh Ahluwalia, founder of the Sikh kingdom. In the Sikh wars of 1845 and 1848-49 they fought against the British, who were struggling to bring the Punjab under control, and who confiscated eighty per cent of their lands. But in 1857, during the Mutiny, Randhir Singh marched his forces into Avadh in support of the imperialists, in the hope that by doing so he might recover his former territory. The British never gave him back the huge tracts whose return he demanded, instead, they rewarded him with a grant of 700 square miles in Kheri and Bahraich in U.P., so that he became one of the biggest taluqdars, or landowners, in the state. When the Maharaja travelled to England in 1870, he met Queen Victoria – always a devotee of Indian princes – and became a favourite at her court; but during the voyage home he fell ill with typhoid fever, and expired at Port Said, aged only forty. Not having expected to die so young, he had made no provision for his younger son, his favourite.

Kharak Singh duly succeeded to the gaddi, or throne, of Kapurthala, but he too died young, poisoned, or carried off by excessive consumption of brandy. In normal circumstances Harnam Singh – Billy's grandfather – would have become the Maharaja, but as a result of palace intrigue, encouraged by the British, he lost the throne and was banished to Jullundur. A later Viceroy, the Earl of Minto, described him as the most distinguished of princes, and reckoned that a great injustice was done to him. Afterwards, as if to make amends, the British created him a hereditary raja, awarded him a knighthood, and granted him the administration of the Avadh properties for his lifetime.

Lonely and dejected, Harnam Singh wandered around Jullundur until he was befriended by a Brahmin who had fled from Bengal when, at the age of nineteen, he became a Christian. This man, who brought Christianity to the Punjab, was originally called Golakhnath Chatterji, but when he settled in Jullundur, hoping to found a church there, the British missionaries called him merely Golakhnath, and persuaded him to give all his children English names. The boys were christened after English kings – William, Henry, Edward – and it was one of his nieces, Priscilla (generally known as Polly, and Indian, in spite of her name) whom Harnam Singh married. She was highly educated, and much cleverer than him, and later wrote papers on the emancipation of Indian women, whereas he had been taught only by English tutors in Kapurthala.

Under the influence of the Golakhnaths, Harnam Singh converted to Christianity, and so destroyed his chances of ever succeeding to the gaddi of Kapurthala – for the British had decreed that no prince might continue to rule if he changed his religion. He lost not only the throne, but also the family jewels. The greatest single piece was the sarpesh, which a maharaja wears on his turban as a badge of office – one very large emerald encrusted with other gems. This was said to have gone to him, but no member of his family has ever seen it again.

Billy remembered his grandfather as having the biggest and most hypnotic eyes that he had ever seen in a human being. No matter that they tended to be slightly bloodshot – perhaps from the large peg of whisky that he enjoyed every evening – even in old age they gave him a formidable appearance. He was also immaculately dressed, and given to wearing fine white kurtas under a black cloak. He was said to change his clothes four times a day, and when he went through his elaborate ritual of dressing in the evening, he always insisted that Billy and his elder brother Jaswant (known as Jumper, because that was how he pronounced his own name) sat with him to watch, eating dalmoth – dried, salted dal.

Billy's sister Amar remembered that to a small child their grandfather always smelt wonderful. She also recalled how formal he was. He disliked shaking hands, and tended to greet people with courtly bows. Her mother had instructed her that when she first saw him in the morning, she must always touch his knees in subservience: when she did, he would brush her hand aside and murmur, 'It's all right.' People were scared of him and would approach obsequiously as he walked up and down, hands behind his back.

Even though they were no longer rulers, the family lived in some style. All Harnam Singh's servants were dressed in the Kapurthala livery of navy blue tunics, white trousers and white turbans with navy bands round them. In the hot weather the entourage would move up to Simla, where they owned the whole top of Summer Hill and lived in the Manor, a fine wooden building set among orchards of apples, apricots and plums.

Jasbir Singh (Billy's father) was born in 1889, the youngest of thirteen children. He was sent first to Forman Christian College, the leading school in Lahore, which was then a flourishing capital city, full of educated people, and regarded by the family as the centre of civilization. He went on to Balliol College, Oxford and enjoyed it immensely, soon becoming popular among his contemporaries. But his career there was not a success, for his prowess was athletic rather than academic. His forte lay in tennis, hockey, football, the pursuit of girls and high living in general, and he lacked intellectual application. Nevertheless, he survived for a while, and financed his extravagances by tutoring the children of well-to-do contacts in golf and tennis, among them two of the adopted sons of the novelist and playwright J.M.Barrie, author of *Peter Pan*. He even – so he told his daughter Amar – sang in pubs to augment his income. He loved English pubs because, in his view, they were 'such equalizers'.

He was eventually sent down – sacked from Oxford – allegedly for tripping up a bulldog (one of the university's private policemen) during a riot. But by then he had made many friends in England, not least with Freddie Lawton, manager of the opera diva Nellie Melba. Among his attributes was a natural bass voice, so fine that Lawton and Melba thought he should develop it professionally and take up an operatic career. But when he wrote to his father suggesting it, he got the regulation telegram with which Harnam Singh was wont to bring his children to heel: CUT YOU OFF WITHOUT A SHILLING.

Instead, Jasbir Singh went to Gray's Inn, in London, where he trained as a barrister and gained full legal qualifications. For a while he lodged with a family called Whiting, in Margate, before returning to India, where he worked as a civil servant. Later he talked of England with enthusiasm, but he never had time to return there – for in his day the trip meant a three-week voyage in each direction.

Billy's mother Mabel was born in 1888, daughter of Eleanor (or Nellie) and Edward Golakhnath. Her childhood was far from easy. Her father, a senior policeman, took to drink and died in Kashmir when she was only two. Her mother married again, this time to an Anglo-Indian named Davis, who according to family tradition was a locomotive driver and lived in Dehra Dun; but she died in childbirth only six years later.

When Mabel, an orphan of about twelve, was seen working as a nanny in a cantonment, the Golakhnaths were so distressed that they brought a legal case to wrest her from the Davis family, and the girl had to go to court to say that she wanted to live with uncle William Golakhnath and aunt Jane, provided they gave her a proper education. This they did, and in due course they sent her to America to be trained as a teacher at the University of Indiana.

Mabel owed a good deal to her foster family, who were highly musical: they all sang beautifully, and played the violin and piano, but later in life she rarely spoke of her early years. Although physically minute – only four feet eleven inches when fully grown – she developed into a formidable character, and she was always secretive by nature – a trait which she passed on to Billy.

She and Jasbir Singh were married on New Year's Eve, 1914, when they were both twenty-five, and in due course had two sons, a daughter and then another son. The eldest, Jaswant, was born in 1915; Billy arrived in 1917, Amar in 1924 and Balram in 1926. Mabel's favourites were always Billy and Balram: according to Amar, she spoiled them rotten, and she retained a powerful influence over both of them, but Billy especially, perhaps because he never married.

Billy's earliest memory is of arriving at Balrampur. His father was appointed special manager of the estate there in 1923 and for the six-year-old boy that posting proved a crucial event, for it planted in him a lifelong fascination with the great forests of northern India, and with the animals that inhabited them.

Situated some 150 miles north-east of Lucknow, and only twenty miles from the border of Nepal, Balrampur was then the largest and richest princely state in the United Provinces. Its nominal ruler was the Maharaja Pateshwari Prasad Singh, but because he was underage, and a congenital idiot, Jasbir Singh was appointed special manager, responsible to the provincial administrative organization known as the Court of Wards, and so became the effective ruler of a private kingdom. No doubt his own princely background was a factor in his selection.

Part of the charm of Balrampur was its remoteness. The town lay twenty-six miles from the city of Gonda, and could be approached by road or rail, both of which ran through forests harbouring many game animals, among them wild boar, chital (spotted deer), muntjac (barking deer) and leopards. When travellers crossed the Rapti river on a pontoon bridge, they often saw marsh crocodiles lying out on sandbanks with their mouths agape to absorb the heat of the sun. There were also gharials – primitive, fish-eating crocodiles up to twenty-five feet long, whose slender snouts were topped (if they were males) by large protuberances resembling a ghara, or earthenware pot.

At Balrampur the manager's house was a lovely old colonial building – very large, made of brick, set in enormous gardens and grounds, equipped with its own cricket pitch and an akhara, or wrestling arena. When the family arrived the only illumination was from gas lamps, but later Billy's father brought in electricity. Everything was done on a princely scale. There was an army of 300 soldiers, including a platoon of Gurkhas and a contingent of cavalry. The estate no longer owned 200 elephants, as it once had, but there were still a good number, which took part in ceremonial parades and were used when the manager wanted to travel around the villages – a slow but impressive means of transport – as well as for tiger beats in the jungle.

The garages housed a whole fleet of big American cars – a Cadillac, Chevrolets, Buicks, a couple of Clevelands. Servants abounded. Billy's father always had a Sikh manservant, but the cooks were Muslims, because they were reputed to be the most skilled in the kitchen. There was an ayah for each of the children, and a manservant for each pair. These men were by no means in awe of their charges: whenever Amar and Balram tried to give their minder orders, he paid no attention except to say, 'Be quiet!'

The job of managing Balrampur was not particularly arduous: it left Jasbir Singh time to be with his family, and the children looked on their father and mother not just as parents, but as companions as well. In his bathroom he would sit in the tub, telling stories and singing Negro spirituals in his fine bass voice, while Jaswant and Billy perched entranced on the wooden thunder-box. Their father would recall how he had heard the great Caruso sing, and how the diminutive tenor would rise on his toes as he hit high notes. He told the boys how Nellie Melba had refused to perform with the Italian, preferring the Irish John McCormack as a partner. Sometimes Mabel accompanied him on the piano, and whenever missionaries arrived from America, they sang *Swing Low, Sweet Chariot* with wonderful harmonies.

One engaging quirk of Jasbir Singh's was his passion for railways. A great admirer of power in any form, he loved the apparently effortless energy that trains seemed to possess, and the smoothness with which they travelled. Wherever he was posted, among the first things he found out were the positions of level crossings in the area: taking the young children with him, he would stay for hours, waiting for trains to pass. The fascination may have derived from the fact that his father had always retained a special carriage for journeys to Lahore, Simla or Delhi.

While the children were young, they spoke to the servants

in Hindi or Urdu, but talked to their parents in English. English ideas and customs permeated the household. Not only had Jasbir Singh been at Oxford, Billy's uncle Shumsher Singh spent twenty-eight years in England and played cricket for the Kent second XI, and his aunt Amrit had been head girl at Sherborne .

In Balrampur the boys were taught by a series of governesses, most of whom were accelerated on their way by the intolerable behaviour of their charges. An American, Miss Bayles, who complained constantly about the food, was soon replaced by the Scottish Miss Anderson, described by Billy as 'a desiccated and cadaverous lady, of an unbelievable thinness, with a parchment complexion'. So fascinated were the boys by her skeletal proportions that they became determined to see her naked, and one day they burst in while she was in the bath tub – out of which she leapt with 'an outraged shriek and incredible agility'. The manoeuvre secured both their aims – to view her skinny figure, and to bring about her immediate resignation.

The result of so much contact with Western ideas was to leave Billy (in his own estimate) with a mind and outlook half-Indian and half-English. As he grew up, he came to realize that the Indian mind is much the more subtle and devious of the two, and he found that his own semi-English directness could sometimes be a handicap. One symptom of his dual nature is the fact that for the rest of his life he has spoken English with a strong Indian accent: unlike his siblings, who sounded perfectly Anglicized, he retained the rhythms and intonations that he learned as a boy. He was also unlucky in the matter of his voice: whereas Balram inherited their father's beautiful bass, Billy suffered from some early throat ailment that made his voice inclined to crack.

Although he had been a wonderfully handsome baby, he was never a robust child. From the age of three he was plagued by stomach trouble, being constantly sick and unable to digest his food. He became so weak that for two years he lost the power of speech, and his mother thought he was going to die. Then at last, when he was about eight, after numerous other remedies had failed, a civil surgeon, Captain Cook, told his mother to try giving him tablets called Parathyroid. These, he said, could do no harm, as they were merely a palliative, but in fact they cured what seems to have been a calcium deficiency.

His father, in contrast, was powerfully built, very keen on physical development, and a good athlete. He excelled at tennis, and twice won the all India doubles championship. Billy's elder brother, Jaswant, took after their father: although short in stature, he too became immensely strong (later known by his contemporaries as 'the pocket Hercules'), and with his good natural eye revelled in athletic sports, scoring a double-century in school cricket, and twice winning the army tennis championships. Billy, in contrast, lacked physical coordination, and resented the fact that his brother was more gifted. One sign of his clumsiness was his handwriting, which has always been so nearly illegible that recipients of letters sometimes claim that the best chance of deciphering them is to pin them on the wall and try to read their mysteries as they run past.

At home, their father's particular passion was for wrestling, and he retained one of the mahouts, or elephant drivers, Sarwar Khan, as an instructor for himself and his sons. On one side of the akhara there was a pile of earth known as Ali's Mound, sacred to Ali, son of the prophet Mohammed, and the patron saint of wrestling, on to which competitors threw earth as they went into the arena; the mud floor was freshly dug-over every morning, and as they wore only loin-cloths, they emerged from bouts slimy with mud and sweat from head to foot.

Every October, during the festival of Dussehra, Jasbir Singh organized a dangal or wrestling tournament to which leading wrestlers were invited from all over India. Among the stars were Kikar Singh, the Sikh who claimed to be so strong that he could pull out a babul tree (acacia) by its roots, and the Chaubeys from Mathura, who were so vast that nobody could turn them over to put them on their backs. Matches took place in the akhara, and spectators were given shelter in a pandal, or large marquee. The winners received cash prizes, as well as brightly-embroidered turbans and scarves, and the fame of the event spread far and wide. The whole tournament was for men only: women were not allowed to watch. Amar was incensed at being excluded, and when she challenged her father, asking 'Why do you do such disgusting things?,' he struck back by saying, 'I don't stop you riding your horse.'

Although never himself a pugilist, Jasbir Singh was fascinated by boxing: he knew the famous referee Eugene Corrie, and had once shaken hands with the legendary Johnson, the first black world heavyweight champion, into whose giant black paw his own small hand disappeared. His talk about such giants infected Billy with the same enthusiasm, which was fanned by the purchase of a series of four books called *Black Dynamite*, all about boxers. Among the boy's early heroes were Homicide Hank, alias Henry Armstrong, who won titles at three weights, bantam, middle and light-heavy, and Jack Dempsey, 'the Manassa Mauler', who had become world heavyweight champion in July 1919.

Billy's mother naturally went in for gentler pursuits. A keen gardener, she kept doves, peacocks and dogs, which she encouraged to dig for rats, and at weekends she would go down with the family for picnics by the Kwana river, one of their favourite resorts. Later in life Billy felt sure that his love of animals derived from her.

Billy's father was thirty-four when he arrived at Balrampur, and until then he had never done any big-game shooting. Because the state forests extended to many thousands of acres, and shooting was the universal recreation for the managers of such properties, he soon took to it with enthusiasm. So did Billy – on a small scale at first, but with a lust for blood that later disgusted and haunted him.

His first accomplice was a boy called Minu Ismail, two years his senior, whose father was a professor at Forman Christian College. Armed with air-guns, the pair prowled the purlieus of the house, 'bloodthirsty and murderous urchins', as Billy himself recalled, 'with an innate desire to slaughter everything in sight'. For much of the time they were out of control, and Billy's mother could not keep track of them.

Not content with blasting geckos off the walls of buildings, they would bombard the frogs that floated on the surface of ponds, killing many but leaving dozens maimed. If Minu was slightly the less vicious of the two, it may only have been because his mother rationed his ammunition to eight slugs a day, whereas Billy's mother issued him with as many pellets for his .177 Diana as he wanted.

With constant practise, he soon developed into what he called 'a deadly little killer', dropping birds of all kinds, including pond herons, egrets, doves and a Brahminy kite. However the least excusable of all his depredations took place in the Balrampur zoo, to which he and his associate would repair in the evenings, when they had finished lessons. At the entrance to the zoo was a museum which housed the skeleton of Chand Murat, an elephant which had stood eleven feet six inches at the shoulder, and was reputed to be the largest-ever Indian pachyderm. This exhibit, being dead, was of little interest to them.

Although too cowardly to take on Prince, the zoo's one tiger, they singled out a leopard that lived in a small cage and bombarded it so relentlessly that it died of lead poisoning. Next they deliberately lamed a flamingo by shooting it in the one leg on which it habitually stood, to see what would happen if they destroyed its normal support. It seems extraordinary that Babu Ram Lochan, who was in charge of the zoo, did not report them to Billy's father: the boys could only conclude that the keeper imagined the inmates were there for entertainment, 'and if it amused the scion of the boss to pepper the animals ... with lead shot, it was not his place to object'.

Minu was a great spinner of yarns, and enjoyed terrifying local children with a fantastical tale about how he had been chased on his bicycle by a pack of wolves, how he had leapt off and with his hands had torn one wolf's jaws asunder. Billy tried to keep his end up by describing how he had been charged by a king cobra, and had slaughtered the snake with a stone, only to become confused by his own inventions and end up in a state of embarrassment.

Minu also liked to relay embroidered versions of news from the great world outside. It was he who brought word of the first million-dollar boxing match in September 1926, when Gene Tunney beat Jack Dempsey over twelve rounds in Philadelphia. A year later, he gave a graphic description of the Battle of the Long Count, when Tunney beat Dempsey again, to retain the heavyweight title in Chicago, amid much dispute: at one point he was on the floor of the ring for at least fifteen seconds, but the referee took so long to begin the count that he was able to recover. The boys' interest in boxing never waned, and even in his twenties Billy hero-worshipped Joe Louis, the Brown Bomber, when he became world heavyweight champion in 1937. Later still he conceived a powerful admiration for Cassius Clay, alias Mohammed Ali, but he remained convinced that the greatest heavyweight of all time was Dempsey, who, although so formidable in the ring, was gentle, mild and good-mannered outside it.

Growing older, the precocious killers became fascinated by the weapons in the estate armoury, and soon could recite the performance of every one – especially after they had acquired a catalogue of rifle ballistics. To this day Billy remembers that the American .30-06 calibre fired bullets of four different weights – 220, 180, 150 and 110 grains – and that the 110-grain bullet had the terrific muzzle-velocity of 3,500 feet per second. The finest rifles, to which every hunter aspired, were the Holland & Holland double-barrelled .375 and .465 magnums, both far more powerful than the ancient .500 black-powder express which his father preferred. Even before they had a chance to fire the heavy weapons, Billy and Minu would spend hours, like two old colonels, discussing the relative merits of light bullets and high muzzle-velocities, which gave flatter trajectories and therefore greater accuracy, as against heavier, slower rounds, which dropped more on the way to the target, but had greater stopping-power.

High on their list of agreeable pastimes were shooting forays in the nearby forests, made in the estate cars. One of the drivers, Mohammed Hussain, was perfectly prepared to halal, or cut the throat of, any edible animal they shot, thus making it fit to be eaten by fellow-Muslims. But their favourite chauffeur was Bechan, who looked like a 'dark and rather shop-soiled edition of Clark Gable', and drove an ancient, off-white Cadillac, at the same time manipulating a searchlight with amazing dexterity. Time and again on nocturnal expeditions the boys fired off at eyes they saw glowing in the dark, leaving many animals wounded. To this day Billy remains haunted by an incident in which they disabled a hyena, ran out of ammunition, tried in vain to kill it by running it over, and in the end drove off, leaving it to die.

Gradually he came to appreciate the vast extent of the forests that surrounded Balrampur and stretched away northwards to the foothills of the Himalayas. To the south lay the Terai, or flat plain, bearing the zamindari forests, which were owned by the various estates and contained relatively low-value timber. To the north was the bhabar – the strip of land, ten or twenty miles from north to south, enriched by alluvial deposits washed down after monsoon rains from the Churia mountains in Nepal. On the bhabar grew some of the great government forests for which the Raj was famous, consisting mainly of Sal, a valuable hardwood tree in constant demand for railway sleepers, beams, girders, rafters, door-frames and so on.

The zamindari forests were full of chota shikar (small game) such as chital and wild boar, which lived on farmers' crops. There was also a good population of leopards. On the other hand, tigers – the ultimate target of every big-game hunter – kept almost entirely to the government forests, in which they regulated their own numbers with extraordinary precision. Whenever a tiger was shot, and a particular territory was left empty, news of the event would somehow travel back by bush-telegraph up the supply-line into Nepal, where the animals were breeding, and a newcomer would move down to take over the vacant space. Billy always remembered how the Bachkahi forest block, where a ravine led down from the mountains, seemed to be equipped 'with a kind of stop-valve, which only allowed a replacement when required.' Thus the supply of tigers seemed never-ending, and nobody had the slightest worry that they might one day be threatened with extinction.

Among the staff at Balrampur, he most revered the shikaris – the hunters and trackers, who built machans, laid out beats and took guests into the forests to shoot. These men were given land next to the jungle, in villages roundabout, and when not working for the estate, spent their time protecting their own crops from the depredations of pigs and deer. Billy envied them, because he imagined – not without some foundation – that they devoted most of their lives to shooting. A particular local hero was Lala Babu, superintendent of the elephant stables, owner of a village in the heart of the forest, and the most brilliant rifle-shot. His prize possession was a beautifully engraved .450/400 double-barrelled rifle, and in Billy's memory it was always a pleasure to sit on a machan with him, as there was a professional touch about everything he did.

Billy was only twelve when he shot his first leopard, and he remembered the occasion ever after. He had been placed in a grass hide, on the ground, to mount guard over a kill some fifty yards away, accompanied by his father's chaprasi, Ragbar Dayal. Being too small to fire a full-bore rifle, he was armed with an old 12-bore shotgun – a smooth-bore weapon which fired cartridges loaded with single balls, and was less accurate and powerful than a rifle. Nevertheless, when the leopard appeared, Billy let drive. The animal gave a great leap, tumbled over and staggered away – and when Ragbar went to look for it, he found it lying dead, shot through the heart. The boy went home cock-a-hoop at having killed a female leopard six and a half feet long.

His first tiger, which he got at the age of fourteen, was less satisfactory. This time he sat and waited on a machan with a borrowed, single-shot .355 rifle as a beat was brought towards him: when a tiger appeared, he fired at it, but the animal turned and raced across in front of a second machan, in which another boy was sitting. The lad fired both barrels of his 12-bore, and clearly hit the tiger, which twisted before it disappeared, giving out a yowl. Next morning an armed forest officer went out and found it dead, with a bullet-hole through its chest – so Billy was credited with it, because one slug from the shotgun had only grazed the animal, and the other had hit it in the back.

Thereafter, on occasions too numerous to remember, he had the thrill of sitting up over a bait in the jungle, often at night, waiting for one of the carnivores to return, or of crouching on a machan as a beat came towards him, with the men – either mounted on elephants or on foot – rattling tin-cans full of stones and yelling at the top of their voices, both to drive animals forward, and to give vent to their own fear.

For the hot weather of 1924, when Billy was seven, the family first moved up to Nainital, the hill-station 6,500 feet above the plains, built round the shores of a lake shaped like a teardrop. On the northern side of the lake was an area of level ground, with games pitches laid out on it, and the buildings which climbed the hillsides were all made of wood. There they stayed in Stanley Hall, one of the two houses owned by the Balrampur estate (the other being Ivy Park, in which the Maharaja lodged). In later years the family stayed at Jubilee Hall, one of the highest houses in the town, and it was at the Metropole Hotel, where tennis tournaments were staged, that Billy first set eyes on Jim Corbett, the legendary hunter-naturalist.

A shy railway official, then in his fifties, Corbett came walking down almost furtively to watch the tennis matches; but ten-year-old Billy, fascinated by his reputation as a killer of maneating tigers and leopards, lost no time in making friends. The result was that Corbett invited him round to his home, Gurney House, every Sunday morning, and there he got to know the other members of the household: Jim's sister Maggie, his half-sister Mary Doyle, and Robin, his cocker spaniel, who took part in several of his most dangerous escapades.

Jim had shot his first maneater nearly twenty years before, in 1907, and was still an active hunter – and so it was that the boy heard at first hand the tales which captivated millions of readers when Corbett brought them together in his book *Maneaters of Kumaon*, published in 1944. His earliest version of that best-seller was *Jungle Stories*, a slim, paper-covered volume which he published in Nainital at his own expense in 1935, and of which he presented Billy with a signed copy. The book was dedicated to the 'hundreds of men, women and children killed by the maneaters of Champawat, Muktesar, Panar, Rudra Prayag, Talla Des (3), Chowgarh (2), Mohan and Kanda' – but soon even that list of places was incomplete, and at the front of Billy's copy, in his small, neat handwriting, the author added the names Chuka and Thak, giving the total of recorded victims as 1,225.

The Champawat maneater, which killed over 400 people, the Bachelor of Powalgarh, the maneating leopard of Rudra Prayag – images of these and other fearsome creatures were burnt into Billy's receptive young mind. Corbett, who had a very soft voice, also taught him some practical skills – among them how to set a gin-trap for a porcupine that had been ravaging their potato-crop – and Billy long regretted that he missed a golden opportunity, when the great hunter once came round with an invitation to take part in the search for a killer leopard, only to find that the boy was out.

Except for Jumper, the Singh family were all avid readers, and their houses were full of books. Jasbir liked biographies (and newspapers), and on the whole preferred fact to fiction, but he had certain favourite authors whose novels he read again and again – Rider Haggard, Conan Doyle, Jeffery Farnol and above all P.G. Wodehouse. He always encouraged his children to read, and indeed made them read every afternoon: they all profited from his regime, particularly Balram, who could tackle any text by the time he was four. Just as his father was always buried in P.G. Wodehouse, so he was absorbed by *Peter Pan*, and when he once said to Amar, 'Twenty-seven today,' it meant he had read the book twenty-seven times (in the end his score reached ninety). To the intense irritation of his sister, he could memorize the contents of a book after a single run-through, and later was able to pass exams without studying: his memory was truly photographic. If challenged by his mother (as he often was) about a book he claimed to have read in a ridiculously short time, he would quote whole sentences back to her. Billy also read voraciously, but like his father stuck to favourites.

~

In 1932, when Billy was fifteen, his father's reign at Balrampur came to a sudden end. For political reasons the British, in the immediate form of the governor of U.P., Sir Malcolm Hailey, decided that the idiot Maharaja should marry the daughter of the commander-in-chief of the Nepalese armed forces, a good-looking and intelligent girl, who was only twelve. By then Pateshwari Prasad Singh was physically adult, but the best efforts by numerous European tutors and companions had borne no results – and he was also rumoured to be impotent. So when Jasbir Singh was asked to sanction the dynastic union, he refused, considering that it would be cruel and immoral to saddle a lively young woman with a half-witted husband. He wrote in protest to the Viceroy but was told that he must sort the matter out with Hailey. Still he would not approve of the proposal, and so he was removed from his post, and summarily transferred to Banaras, where he became deputy commissioner. The marriage went ahead, but the British machinations ultimately proved futile, for the young Maharaja simply ran away from his bride and hid.

Jasbir Singh's departure from Balrampur was a highly-charged occasion. As the train stood in the station at Gonda, ready to leave, four or five hundred people thronged the platform, most of them in tears, such was their affection for the man who had looked after them with sagacity and benevolence for the past decade. In Amar's memory, her father was so overcome with emotion that for a while he – who had always taught his children to maintain a stiff upper lip – could not face the crowd. Then her mother told him, 'You'll have to come out,' and in the end he did. When the train began to move, people ran after it with tears streaming down their faces, clinging to the final moments of the old regime.

Billy, too, was deeply moved that day. As the engine hauled the train out of the station, with its heavy heartbeats gradually picking up steam, through the windows he watched all the stalwarts of his father's regime pass slowly before his eyes. His anguish was complete when his eye fell on his old guru, Lala Babu, and he imagined him walking back to his grass hut in his village (which Billy himself had visited) in the forest of Bankatwa, with his favourite .450/400 rifle in his hand.

Later, when Billy and Jaswant re-visited the scene of their

father's reign, the people beseeched them to return and take care of them again. Billy looked back on his ten years at Balrampur as a halcyon period, the happiest of his life: he remembered the crackly 78-rpm records of Caruso belting out *On With the Motley;* his father singing *Ol' Man River* in his rolling bass; Douglas Fairbanks swinging from the chandeliers in the jerky, silent black-and-white film of *The Thief of Baghdad* which he saw on a family outing to Lucknow; the magnificent physique of Elmo Lincoln, the Tarzan of the day; the wrestling tournaments in the akhara.

But above all he remembered the shikar, and the intense excitement of hunting the great Indian carnivores in the jungle. He had won accolades for his precocity in shooting a leopard and a tiger, and an elephant, Arjan Bahadur (Arjan the Brave), had been named after him. He already had enormous admiration for the big cats, and knew a good deal about them

His father – never so bloodthirsty – had already renounced shooting, after sitting up over a kill one evening in wait for a leopard. Presently a leopard appeared – but then there came a second, a third and a fourth, and Jasbir was so moved by the sight of the great cats eating and playing that, in Billy's words, 'he returned the old hammer .500 Express to the armoury and never picked up a rifle again'. Around the same time Billy's other mentor, Jim Corbett, was turning from killer to conservationist. It took Billy himself another twenty years to complete his own conversion, but the magic of the jungle and its creatures had entered into his soul, and his sojourn at Balrampur shaped his destiny.

THREE

LEARNING THE ROPES

School never held much fascination for Billy. Being endowed with more than adequate intelligence, he went through the hoops, and passed the necessary exams, often with credit. His mind though was more often outside the classroom than in it, and he always hankered after the great outdoors. He was fifteen when his parents left Balrampur, and they gave him the option of going to Bishop Cotton School in Simla – where he could have lived with his family when they were there on holiday – or to Philander Smith College in Nainital. He chose the second, influenced by the fact that Jim Corbett had been a pupil there, and that Busher, the principal, had been one of Jim's classmates.

His father arranged for him to lodge with the headmaster, F.G. Brandon, known to the boys as 'Barney' – a scholarly teacher but also a strict disciplinarian, famous for the wristy follow-through with which he wielded a cane. Although he had no children of his own, two nephews lodged with him, giving Billy some company, and all three of them were delighted when Barney called them into his study every evening for a communal practice with their yo-yos, the current craze.

To them, but not to him, there was something ridiculous about the way their erudite mentor could not make his yo-yo run up its string, while theirs shot up and down like snakes.

Racism and snobbery were rampant in the school: Anglo-Indian boys spoke freely of 'niggers' and 'nigs', and talked of England as if it were home. As Billy remembered, 'the darker their complexion, the more vociferous they were in talking of British relations,' and a boy called Keelan, though darker than any 'nig', regaled friends with talk of his Scottish descent.

PSC (as Philander Smith College was known) had strong athletic and sporting traditions, especially in soccer and hockey; but Billy, not being good enough at games to represent the school, sought to build up his strength by weight-training, which he did under instruction.

In school, he studied Shakespeare's *Twelfth Night* and *The Tempest*, and read a good deal of poetry, finding he had an accurate memory for quotations that appealed to him. Favourite passages lodged in his mind for the rest of his life, and he never ceased to enjoy quoting them, especially when they became apposite to his work – for instance Wordsworth's

> One impulse from a vernal wood
> May teach you more of man,
> Of moral evil and of good,
> Than all the sages can.

One of his regrets was that he never learned Latin, which – he later realized – is indispensable in the accurate classification of birds and animals. Nor did he make much progress in written Urdu, which was also on the curriculum. English remained his mother tongue, although he became fluent in Hindustani, the mixture of Hindi and Urdu used in everyday speech. In search of an outlet for his creative feelings, he decided to write a treatise on shikar, but soon gave up, disconcerted to find that all he could do was transcribe passages from one of his favourite books, A.A. Dunbar Brander's *Wild Animals of Central India*.

When his parents rented a house in Nainital called Kumaon Lodge, some way below PSC, he went to live there, and had to trudge up the hill to school every morning. Presently Amar and Balram joined the kindergarten under a powerful and eccentric teacher, Miss Mooney, and lunch for all three Singh children was sent up daily in a tiffin-carrier, which kept the food warm. Billy, ashamed at being seen in such juvenile company, generally ate his at a distance. Once, as he looked down out of his classroom window on the top floor of the building, he was delighted to see the entire kindergarten troop out on to the hillside, where, as a punishment for some misdemeanour, they went down on hands and knees, like infant Nebuchadnezzars, and crawled about cropping the grass with their teeth. 'While the great lammergeiers quartered the skies above Laria Kanta,' he remembered in triumph, 'my sister and brother chewed grass below!'

Meanwhile Jaswant, who was hell-bent on a career in the army, had been doing well at the Royal Indian Military College in Dehra Dun, excelling at games and generally making himself popular. When he came to Nainital for a few days' break, he and Billy played football on the tennis court, their teams consisting largely of the coolies employed to carry their mother up hill and down dale in a contraption known as a dandy which was borne on the shoulders of four men.

Among the Singhs' neighbours at Kumaon Lodge was F.W. Champion, a forest officer who wrote and illustrated two outstanding books, *With a Camera in Tigerland* and *The Jungle in Sunlight and Shadow,* and his example perhaps nudged Billy a few steps farther along the road to conservation. Yet when the boys went on holiday to Banaras, they behaved disgracefully, and reverted to their deplorable habits of loosing off their airguns shooting at anything that moved. Balram, using a cast-off weapon of Billy's, was amused by the way goats flicked their tails when he peppered them; and when the old woman looking after the animals remonstrated, he shot her in the leg — an outrage swiftly punished by their father.

Banaras (now Varanasi) was then a filthy place, renowned as the sacred city of the Hindus, and famous for its burning ghats along the banks of the Ganges. For Billy and his family, its chief attraction lay in the presence of the Maharaj Kumar of Vizianagram, known as 'Vizzy', or even as 'Fizzy Vizzy', from his predilection for champagne. (His title denoted that he was the son, but not the heir, of a Maharaja.)

Vizzy's elder brother was the ruler of a state in the south of India, but he himself had settled in Banaras and lived in an elegant palace, whose entrance compound was guarded by an array of full-mounted tigers standing in niches round the walls. The palace grounds included a full-sized cricket field, modelled on the London Oval, for the owner was addicted to the game, and although no great player himself, he had at some stage been taught by those two giants: Jack Hobbs and Herbert Sutcliffe, who had opened the innings for England in countless Test matches. The matchlessly elegant Hobbs, with his record of 196 centuries in first-class cricket, was one of Vizzy's heroes, and when he came out to stay at the palace in Banaras, he became one of Billy's also.

Excitement among local cricket fans ran high when the famous MCC (Marylebone Cricket Club) team arrived from England on tour in January 1934. The side was captained by D.R. Jardine, who had become notorious through his ruthless application of bodyline bowling in Australia during the previous winter, and great was the delight of local cricket fans when Vizzy's XI became the only team to beat the visitors.

The tourists arrived tired after a long overnight journey from Calcutta, but their bowlers tore into the home team with such determination that in their first innings the whole side was out for only 124, of which Vizzy made seventeen. His own bowlers then struck back, dismissing the MCC for a paltry 111. In the second innings the Yuvraj (Crown Prince) of Patiala – a splendidly handsome young man – hit out for a whirlwind forty-four. Jardine was furious, and it was said that when the skipper came in, he instructed his fast bowler E.W. 'Nobby' Clark to 'bowl at the Maharaj Kumar's bloody head!' The order may have had some effect, for this time Nobby, running in with his lovely, fluent action, did dismiss Vizzy for only two runs, but the Vizianagram XI managed to set the MCC a target of 154, and got them out for 139, winning by fourteen runs.

In the evening, after the match, there was the customary dance, at which Jardine was supposed to lead off on the floor with the wife of the governor of U.P., Sir Malcolm Hailey. Unfortunately Jardine – a bloody-minded fellow at the best of times – ignored Lady Hailey, a leathery old Italian, and, defying objections from Billy's father, selected the prettiest girl he could see.

Cricket, however, was of only moderate interest to Billy. More to the point for him was Vizzy's obsession with shikar, his passion for shooting tigers, and his splendid armoury. The contact with Vizzy had a far-ranging effect on Billy's life, for it was through the Maharaj Kumar that he first heard of the forests of North Kheri, the district in which he eventually settled, and in particular of the local state of Singahi, which arranged shoots for British officials.

His curiosity and ambition were awakened when he learnt that Vizzy had taken Jardine to North Kheri for a shoot, and that, staying at a forest rest house called Chhanga Nala, the party had killed five tigers in five days. Ten years passed before Billy headed for the area, but once there, he stayed for life. (Altogether Vizzy claimed a personal total of 383 tigers, but in the end the big cats of Singahi got the better of him, for one of them, a tigress which he had wounded, charged his elephant in a sugar cane field, so that he fell off, ruptured a kidney and died.)

In 1934 Billy took his Senior Cambridge examination for his school-leaving certificate, and, largely as a result of the pressure which his mother had put on him to work, he came not only first in his class, but first in the British Empire – the zenith, he afterwards reckoned, of his scholastic achievement. When his father was transferred from Banaras to Saharanpur as deputy commissioner, he moved to the Lucknow Christian College, where he studied for university and continued his weight-lifting, now according to the principles of Dynamic Tension, laid down by the American bodybuilder Charles Atlas, who was all the rage. He also took a wrestling course under the guidance of Ted Mumby, an American athlete and physical training instructor. The result of all this specialized exercise was that he built up an extremely powerful physique, which served him well when he began his association with big cats, for his sheer strength meant that he was never afraid of any leopard or tiger, and they, sensing this, never showed aggression against him.

Jaswant, meanwhile, had graduated to the Indian Military Academy at Dehra Dun, the training establishment for army officers. There he became an outstanding cadet, winning his colours in four university sports and passing out at as a colour sergeant at his final annual parade. His gifts included energy, good looks and a fine singing voice, as well as a talent for acting and mimicry: he was altogether attractive and well-liked, not least by girls.

Billy later concluded that these natural attributes reduced Jaswant's enthusiasm for hunting – in other words, he believed his elder brother was so talented that he was 'able to achieve competitive excellence unassisted', and had no need 'to prove himself through the destruction of trophy animals'. In less fortunate individuals, among whom Billy classed himself, the compulsive desire to kill animals was 'a deep complex of redirected aggression triggered by insufficiency'. In his own case, to his lasting shame, he concluded that a sickly childhood and a natural lack of talent had made him try to prove himself in society by the indiscriminate slaughter of wildlife – an analysis with which not everyone might agree, but one which, once he had turned the corner to conservation, he applied ruthlessly to himself for the rest of his days.

For the time being, though, he carried on shooting, especially at Christmas camps in the extensive forests that lay between Saharanpur and Dehra Dun. These expeditions were large family gatherings, with much jollity and singing round a log fire every evening. The idea was that the young men should shoot junglefowl for the pot, but they proved so incompetent that everyone was quickly reduced to a vegetarian diet, and their father had to pick up his gun, which he had renounced years before in Balrampur. His brother, Billy's uncle Dalip, once distinguished himself by firing his shotgun at a swarm of bees, and although relatively few of them were knocked down by the pellets, the survivors were irritated enough to attack the rest of the party. Even Billy's aunt B, a non-violent disciple of

Gandhi, entered into the spirit of things by shooting a wild pig – the only animal she ever killed.

In purely intellectual terms, Balram was proving the star of the family. He was sent to Doon School in Dehra Dun – whose founder-principal, A.E. Foot, had been a science master at Eton. Another master, John Martyn, had taught at Harrow, and the staff included several more distinguished scholars. Flourishing in the academic atmosphere, Balram signed the school honours book eleven times, and in due course went on to St Stephen's College in Delhi, where he got a First in history and won blues in four different sports.

Billy, operating at a lower intellectual level, scraped through his Intermediate exam at the second attempt and went to Allahabad University, where he read English, history and economics. Again, weightlifting and wrestling dominated his curriculum (he was once nearly squashed by an immense Sikh, who lay on top of him and was so heavy that he could not move), and at bayonet drill in the University Training Corps he was stabbed by his opposite number. In spite of these setbacks, he passed his Bachelor of Arts exam. His parents had promised that if his marks were good enough, they would reward him by sending him to Oxford – and he very much wanted to go; but in the event his scholastic achievement was only moderate, and by the time he would have gone, World War II had broken out, so that travel to Europe had become impossible.

Putting the idea of Oxford behind him, he sat the examination for the Indian Police, and did pretty well in the written papers, coming fourteenth out of 300-odd entrants, but botched his interview by revealing his ignorance of the Polish Corridor, the vital strip of territory leading to the port of Danzig (now Gdansk) which Hitler was claiming, and by declaring that his favourite author was P.G. Wodehouse – not realizing that the creator of the immortal Jeeves was in disgrace for having made broadcasts which apparently sympathized with the Nazis.

When the British prime minister, Neville Chamberlain, declared war on Germany, on 3 September 1939, Billy volunteered to join the army, never suspecting that the conflict would last nearly six years. He signed up not because he had any feeling of patriotism, but rather because he saw opportunities for travel, and also because he was influenced by his brother's example. He was accepted for a wartime commission, and after a five-month crash-course at the Indian Military Academy in Dehra Dun, learning what it had taken Jaswant two and a half years to assimilate, he was posted to do a gunnery course at the School of Artillery at Kakul, close to Abbottabad (now in Pakistan).

At Kakul, high in the mountains, he found the technicalities of gunnery absorbing: it gave him a sense of power to direct shells on to the opposite slopes and see them blast craters out of the rock. The relationship between officer cadets and instructors was more relaxed than in the infantry, and he soon decided that he preferred firing big guns to being chased about the parade ground by drill sergeants. On 28 December 1940 he was posted to the 'A' Field Regiment, a horse-drawn unit stationed at Deolali, and it was there, a few months later, that he had his first serious altercation with the army.

Before going on a PT (physical training) course, he was told by his troop commander (an Indian) that at the end of it he would be allowed some leave. When the course finished, he sent the troop commander a telegram saying that he was going on leave as arranged, only to receive an angry retort from the British officer commanding his battery, demanding his return.

He scuttled back to Kakul, to be greeted by a rocket, which left him nursing a sense of grievance. He later realized that his chagrin was misguided, but at the time he sought the advice of an Indian officer who had been seconded to the regiment. This man reckoned that the battery commander had made an anti-Indian move, and advised Billy to complain to Brigadier Dennis, Commander of the Royal Artillery of the 17th Division, a friend of his father's who had sponsored his entry into the gunners in the first place.

Dennis blew up, and the upshot was that Billy was placed on Adverse Report, which automatically disqualified him from going on active service with the First Field Regiment when it was deployed to Burma. His disappointment was intense, especially as the regiment had just been issued with brand-new 25-pounder guns and Spider Karrier four-wheel-drive towing vehicles,. Demoted to the Second Indian Anti-Tank regiment in Hyderabad, he was again left behind a few months later when they too went off on active service, and he finished up in the Fifth Maratha Anti-Tank regiment, which had recently converted from infantry and had totally inadequate equipment. It was with this unit that he eventually went abroad, once the term of his Adverse Report had run out.

On their way to join the Tenth Indian Army as part of the PAI (Persia and Iraq Force), the Fifth Anti-Tank were temporarily stationed at Babina, in Jhansi, and Billy had a chance to go and say goodbye to his father in Lucknow, where Jasbir had become Deputy Commissioner (the first Indian to hold the post). As they parted at the station, he told Billy, 'Do your best. I know you will never falter or fail.' Billy never forgot how 'reassuring and indestructible' his father looked as the train steamed out: he had no intimation that he would never see him again.

Billy was twenty-four, and this was his first trip abroad. His regiment sailed from Bombay to Basra, on the north-west shore of the Persian Gulf, and made camp in the desert at Zubair, a dozen miles from the Shatt-el-Arab, the confluence of the Tigris and the Euphrates. The heat, the flies, the endless sandy wastes and the gritty dust that penetrated every crevice made them wonder why they were occupying such a godforsaken area of the globe, and Billy wholeheartedly endorsed the feelings of a British other-rank who wrote home to his family, 'I am not allowed to say where we are, but I am at the arsehole of the world and gradually travelling up it.'

Things improved slightly when they moved to Musaiyab, close to Baghdad, and they could occasionally sample the delights of the capital's red-light district. In July 1942, when the great battle of El Alamein was raging in the Western Desert, orders came that they were to proceed to the area as reinforcements; but when the authorities realized that they were armed only with obsolete World War I guns, and needed to borrow transport to move them, the instructions were countermanded.

Still stuck outside Baghdad, Billy was hit by a thunderbolt: a telegram from Jaswant told him that their father had died suddenly of typhoid, aged fifty-three. The news seemed impossible to believe. Billy retired to his tent and, by his own account, 'wept inconsolably'. An attempt to drown his despair with whisky failed when he was wretchedly sick, but he obtained a month's compassionate leave and hurried back to Lucknow, where he found his family overwhelmed by the tragedy. He learnt that his father had died intestate, leaving Mabel to clear the necessary financial documents and find somewhere to live. His death also left her short of money: from having always been well-off, the family suddenly found itself short of funds. Deprived of her husband's support and company, Mabel felt very vulnerable, and begged Billy not to challenge authority any more.

Attempting to return to his unit, he had to wait several weeks for accommodation on a ship, and so involuntarily overran his leave by nearly a month. This caused more ill feeling, and his commanding officer accused him of having conspired with the shipping authorities so that he could spend Christmas at home. When the regiment was ordered to move up to Sultanabad, in Persia, en route for Teheran, Billy escorted the guns on a train heading north, and was relieved to climb into the mountains, away from the heat and insects of the desert. Two months later he was on his way south again: the deployment to Teheran had been cancelled, and once more he was detailed to take charge of the heavy weapons.

This time they loaded their equipment on to a paddle-steamer, embarked at Awaz, and for ten days proceeded slowly down the river of that name. Yet again Billy reverted to earlier habits. Herds of small desert gazelle congregated on the banks of the river, and from their floating machan the officers blazed away at them with rifles. As Billy recalled in old age:

> The day resounded to incessant rifle fire, and at night we drank whisky by moonlight, interrupting the proceedings now and then to let loose a fusillade at ghostly figures flitting in the moonlight. What we killed, we picked up; the wounded were left. It was a disgusting exhibition of compulsive slaughter, and I now shudder at the memory of it.

During the voyage they heard that their unit had been attached to the celebrated Fourth Indian Division, which was fighting in Burma. At last it seemed that, after a refit, they would really go to war. But it was not to be. As soon as they reached India, their orders were cancelled, and they were retained on garrison duties in Ranchi.

By then Billy had had enough of the army. He did not get on with his commanding officer, and disliked many of his colleagues. He felt that all his gunner training had been wasted. Irritations abounded at every level. What rankled most was his knowledge that he had brought himself to a low pass through his own intransigence. He therefore applied for a transfer to the Indian Air Force (in which Jaswant was having outstanding success), or to some civilian occupation, his excuse being that he had been passed over for promotion.

His reward was to be put on Adverse Report a second time, and summoned to an interview in Delhi. On the way he looked in on Major General Frank Moore, then in command of 14 Division, who had employed Jim Corbett to train British soldiers in jungle warfare. Moore was sympathetic, spoke warmly of Jaswant, whom he had helped in the past, and wrote to Army Headquarters, offering to take Billy into his division – all to no avail.

At an interview with the military secretary, Billy was given the choice of resigning or being cashiered. In desperation he wrote to his mother, saying he was about to be thrown out of the army: could she get him an interview with Sir Claude Auchinleck, the Commander-in-Chief? She herself went to see the boss, and found him wonderfully civil.

'Khorani Sahib,' he said, 'I'd love to be able to countermand the order, but these reports really give me no loophole.' When he gave a chuckle, Mabel said sharply, 'I must tell you, this is no laughing matter' – to which he replied: 'Whatever you do, don't put him into any service that demands obedience. He doesn't know the meaning of the word.'

Billy's siblings, meanwhile, had been enjoying mixed

fortunes. Easily the most successful was Jaswant, who had done a year's attachment to the British Royal Fusiliers, where he trained the regimental hockey team. He was then posted to the 4/12 Frontier Force Regiment and saw action at Fort Jamrud against the Pathans. For two years in succession he won the Indian Army tennis championships, and was then transferred to the air force, where he flew fighters (ferrying some to Canada) and as a squadron leader carried out bombing sorties.

Balram, having excelled intellectually at school and university, also tried to join the air force, but was mortified to be rejected on the grounds that, although he was the same height as Jaswant, his legs were too short for him to become a pilot. In vain he pointed out that the World War II fighter ace Douglas Bader had no legs at all, having lost them in a crash, and that, even before the accident, he had been very short. Because Balram was sponsored by Micky Nethersole, an air ace in the World War I, and by the 1940s was high in the Indian Civil Service, the case attracted a lot of publicity, and this made it impossible for the authorities to reverse their decision, but Balram always reckoned that it ruined his life.

His mother advised him to try for the army, but that did not appeal, and when he was rejected by the navy, he went straight from university into business in Calcutta, joining the firm of Balmer Laurie, which traded in tea and other commodities, and so becoming a boxwallah.

Of the four children, Amar had by far the most difficult early life, because although she was devoted to her father, and adored by him, she did not get on with her mother. It seemed to Amar that Mabel had somehow never expected to have a daughter, and did not know how to deal with her. The problem – she thought – stemmed from the difficulties that Mabel herself had experienced as a child, and there was always tension between them. It seemed to Amar that her mother was always demanding, and critical of her, holding her on a tight rein and not allowing her to go to parties. In the end she escaped to the Isabella Thoburn College in Lucknow, an American missionary establishment for Indian girls, where she studied history, economics and civics. Even then she was not entirely free. She wanted to live in college, with her friends, but her mother insisted on her remaining at home, with the result that she had to bicycle in and out every day, escorted by a family retainer – a long ride across the river. Luckily she had inherited the Golakhnath talent for music, and when a visiting American called Alice Jefferson (a descendant of President Thomas Jefferson) heard her play the piano, she got her a scholarship to major in piano studies at the Eastman School of Music at Rochester University. So, at the age of nineteen, Amar followed in her mother's footsteps to America.

There she enjoyed herself: she had got away from her mother, and made many friends, and she met the celebrated English pianist Myra Hess. Having heard Amar play, the great lady offered to give her lessons in England, if it suited her. When her course ended, Amar had no wish to return and live with her mother, who had bought a house in Lucknow. She therefore went to London for the time being, hoping that she might eventually get a job teaching in Delhi. But when Mabel came to England to discuss her future, it was decided that she should learn shorthand, typing and public speaking, which she did.

In 1952, when she was twenty-eight, she married an Englishman, John Commander – a move which, she later said, cost her 'a terrible price'. Her first child, Simon, was born in 1954, but in 1958, when her second, Priya, was on the way, the marriage broke up through mutual distaste, and she was left to fend for herself. After various part-time editorial jobs, she joined the staff of the India Office Library as a research assistant where she succeeded Stella Rimington (later head of the intelligence agency MI5), and she gradually built a scholarly reputation as researcher and author, with particular expertise on the history and affairs of Tibet and Bhutan. Although she opted to live in London, she has kept up regular visits to India over the years, and has stayed with Billy at Tiger Haven more times than she can count.

FOUR

FARMER

With the war coming to an end, Billy found himself cast adrift, all too well aware that he had failed to carry out his father's last instructions. Told that he must neither falter nor fail, he had done both, and now he had no powerful advocate to bail him out. What could he do?

He applied half-heartedly for one or two jobs in business, knowing that in truth he would find office routine insupportable, and tried with more determination for a post in the forest service. Unfortunately, his academic qualifications were not good enough, and at twenty-eight he was already too old to be accepted. At that stage he had no interest in trees or conservation, but supposed that a job in forestry would at least bring him some shooting. It was the animals of the forest that attracted him, and if a separate wildlife service had existed, he would have gone for it; but then, as now, wildlife was treated as a lowly department of forestry, and no jobs were available on that front.

Then at last fate seemed to take a hand, when he happened to meet Jai Singh, younger brother of the Raja of Bijwa, a small feudal state near the Nepalese border. Jai had just started farming on land leased from George Hearsey, a descendant of General Sir John Hearsey, Commander of the British Army in West Bengal, who had quelled an incipient mutiny at Barrackpore in 1857. Billy was in awe of the legendary courage displayed by the general, who – by one account – ordered the troops out on parade, marched out alone from the saluting base, drew his revolver, shot dead the ringleader of the dissidents, Mangal Pandey, turned about, and went back to his place without looking behind him. The troops were so overawed that they surrendered their arms (although thereafter all mutineers were known as 'Pandeys'), and the general was rewarded by a huge grant of land in U.P.

Jai spoke of the joys and problems of agriculture in North Kheri, which he called 'the Chicago of the East': there was unlimited land available, he said, and the shooting was phenomenal. Other well-wishers told Billy that, whatever happened if he became a farmer, he would not starve. He stayed with the Raja on his farm, and when he went out with him along the Sarda river, which flows down out of the Himalayas, they heard the hooves of countless swamp deer thundering through the tamarisk on the river banks. In the evening they sat up over the carcass of a buffalo killed by a tigress, and later drank whisky out of tooth-mugs. In the warm darkness the frustrations of army life painlessly evaporated, and the prospect of working the soil in such surroundings seemed so alluring that Billy went to the nearby town of Pallia and leased a 750-acre plot of virgin land.

When someone warned him that hundreds, if not thousands, of wild pig and deer would compete with him for possession, he saw himself as 'the holder of a thin red line,' and bought a .275 Mauser rifle with which to defend his property. Thus equipped, he became a farmer.

On 30 April 1945 he took the night train from Lucknow, where his mother was living, and at 3.30 the next morning stepped down on to the platform at Pallia Kalan, a one-horse halt five miles short of the Nepalese border. As he loaded his luggage onto the wooden bullock cart which was waiting for him, the train pulled away to the north, and he set out to walk three miles to the site he had chosen for a house, along a dusty dirt road lit by a waning moon and bright stars. Away to his right a fox gave a chattering bark, and closer at hand a pack of jackals sang their falsetto chorus: *Dead Hindu, dead Hindu. Where are you?*

He had not selected the place for its scenic beauty: most of the scrub land around was flat as a chapatti, but at one point it rose a few feet, and he had picked this slight eminence for his base because it commanded a view over the immediate surroundings. He had decided to call his homestead Jasbirnagar (Jasbir's place), in memory of his father.

By the time he reached the spot, the sky was paling. In front of him a hog deer bolted, giving out thin alarm whistles, and the grunts of a leopard – in and out, in and out: like the sound of a man sawing wood – told him what had frightened it.

Dawn revealed grassland stretching away to the west in a limitless sea of herbage, much of it ten feet high. On an open patch which the ungulates had grazed down stood a herd of twenty nilgai, India's largest antelope – ungainly creatures the size of small horses, yet of a quite different shape, with pointed faces, humped withers and sloping rumps. Beyond them grazed a herd of blackbuck, smaller antelopes easily identified by their ribbed and spiralling horns. The horns of domestic cattle and buffalo glinted in the early light. The talk of competition had not been exaggerated.

As no house existed, Billy got some labourers to build him

a chappar – a thatched grass hut. Because he had heard that the men tended to be idle, he stood over them, staying out in the sun until he collapsed with a severe attack of heat-stroke. He lived in that grass hut for the next nine years, in what most people would have considered intolerable discomfort. Without electricity, there was no air-conditioning – not even any fans – and in summer the temperature was often over 110° F in the shade. Although plenty of water was available – for the water table lay only a few feet below ground level, and he had tapped it with a 200-foot well – there was no piped supply.

When Amar once came to stay for a few days, she found the privations appalling. To her horror she noticed that the cook's bare back was crawling with flies. The thunderboxes were so revolting that when she needed – as Billy put it – to answer a call of nature, she went off into the fields, only to find that the farmhands stared at her uninhibitedly. 'The bathing arrangements were quite dreadful,' she remembered. 'You had two buckets, and two men would come and hold up a sheet and look the other way. I used to say, "Billy – suppose they turn round?" "Oh," he said, "so what? You fuss too much."'

Perhaps she did. Yet even Billy admitted that his life was tough and lonely, and that it was only his 'natural perversity of character' that enabled him to endure it. The area was far from hospitable, being infested not only with malaria-carrying mosquitoes, but also with dacoits, or bandits, who lived illegally in the forest, brazenly taking over the rest houses when the staff of the forest department left them for the rainy season, and terrorizing local people so effectively that whole villages had been abandoned. In the late 1940s the chief dacoit was a former convict and wrestler called Bashira, who robbed and murdered at will. As Billy remarked, 'Might was right in the land, and the strong oppressed the weak.'

He himself was anything but weak. He did, as a concession, build a small house of brick for his cook, and he planted numerous trees around the site: sal, the prime timber tree which grew high and handsome in the forest to the north, never did well, but shisham, ashokas, bauhinias, pipal, khair and teak flourished, and as they grew they transformed Jasbirnagar into a pleasant grove, dappled with light and shade.

In the early days he bought some buffaloes and a plough, and put in paddy as a crop for the coming monsoon – but no sooner had the first shoots come up than the antelopes and deer moved in to eat them off. So too did the gaddis, or muslim graziers, whose cattle and buffaloes had until then enjoyed unlimited access to the land, and now found cultivated crops much to their taste.

Before long Billy became enraged by the sight of two bullocks grazing in one of his fields. Because they were too wild to catch, he deliberately lamed them by shooting them in the knee with his .22 rifle. With the animals' manoeuvrability reduced, he managed to capture both, and sent them to the local cattle pound, but then made the bad mistake of confessing what he had done to the local vet, at the same time asking him to treat the casualties.

The owner promptly started legal action, and Billy was summoned to appear before a magistrate at Lakhimpur, fifty-five miles away along appalling roads. The local newspaper took up the story, trumpeting that a thug from the army had outraged Hindu sensibilities by shooting sacred cows without provocation. He managed to settle out of court, bought the injured animals, and, when they had recovered, sold them for more than he paid. He therefore considered he had won the first round in his struggle with the gaddis – and although many more altercations ensued, 'by a mixture of cajolery and strong-arm tactics' he held his own.

Sometimes Billy would spend a few days in Lucknow, to be with his mother, who had rented an old colonial house at 98, The Mall. There she had made a lovely garden, but she was lonely after Jasbir Singh's death, and enjoyed having members of the family to stay. There, one day in 1947, Billy once again saw Jim Corbett, who, with a heavy heart, had decided to move to Africa.

Corbett, then seventy-two, had conceived the idea that after Independence everything would change, that any Britons who remained in India would be persecuted, and that he, a foreigner, would no longer be welcome in the country to which he had devoted his life. In this he was tragically wrong, for no one in the hills of Kumaon – the area he had patrolled – was better loved than he. Nevertheless, he was going, and he had come to Lucknow to say goodbye to Mrs Naidu, the Governor. As No. 98 was more or less opposite Government House, he walked across to see the Singhs and tell them he was off to Tanganyika, to farm with two other partners, Percy Wyndham and Robert Bellaires. 'None of us has any children,' he told Billy. 'Why don't you come and manage the farm with us, and then take it over?'

The idea had its attractions, and Billy was swayed by the high regard in which he held his old mentor; but he was too deeply involved in his own operations to make such a drastic change, and had to decline.

In 1949 Mabel left 98, The Mall and moved to a villa at 3, Oliver Road. Later she went to live with Jaswant and his wife Mariam, until Jaswant's untimely death in 1962. Then she alternated between Balram in Calcutta, Billy's home Tiger Haven in winter, and Dehra Dun in the hot weather.

In Kheri, the purchase of a small, three-wheeled tractor, a John Deere Model B, enabled Billy to extend his cultivations, and when his farming operations began to yield a small income, he turned his attention to the nearby forests. The North Kheri forest division was a commercial, working forest, from which valuable timber was sold by auction to private contractors. The division was also organized for sport shooting, and outsiders could apply to rent individual blocks. Each successful applicant was allowed to shoot specified numbers of game animals, as well as to rent one of the forest houses for the duration of its permit, and Billy began organizing Christmas parties very much on the lines of the ones his father had held before the war.

Most of the arrangements, in fact, were made by his mother, who was extremely practical: in those days there was no shop in Pallia, and every item of food, drink and equipment needed for a ten-day stay had to be brought out from Lucknow or Delhi. The main family party came down by train, travelling in a reserved, first-class compartment which had its own lavatory, with the cook, bearers and other servants in second class. At Pallia halt Billy would meet them with his jeep, and bullock-carts and maybe an elephant would be waiting to transport the mountain of stores – rice, dal, whisky, soda, oil for the lamps and so on – into the jungle.

Every camp was an adventure, for it took place in the heart of the forest, far from civilization, surrounded by wild animals. As Billy himself recorded, the gatherings were reunions of family and friends rather than serious shooting expeditions; nevertheless, 'the old urge for slaughter' was still smouldering in him, 'and the destruction of the master predator (the tiger) dominated all desires'. Soon a regular ritual developed. To everyone's amusement, Jaswant would turn up on his own, coming directly from whatever air force base he was stationed at. Then his wife Mariam, offspring of a Pathan father and a Scots mother (according to Kipling, the ideal mixture), would arrive with their two children and a mountain of luggage. Both Jaswant and Mariam were greatly loved by the rest of the family – she because of her high spirits and sense of fun, he because he could get on with anyone, in spite of his aristocratic background, and, when on leave, relaxed completely, identifying with the servants and helping them with their tasks.

Balram, also immensely convivial, often brought bachelor friends from Calcutta, until in 1955 he married Mira Benjamin, an elegant and lively girl from a Christian family, very well educated, who had lived in Harrow-on-the-Hill, and had been to a private school there, while her father was posted to the Indian High Commission in London. Once they were married, Balram brought her (and later their two sons, Jasmer and Karanbir) to the camps. Mira was at first startled by the way of life in the forest and the boisterous family jokes: a town person, she never cared for shooting, but she came to love the expeditions, which introduced her to the jungle. Amar sometimes completed the family party by coming out from England with her two children.

When Billy acquired his own elephant and a reliable car, he was able to set up the camps in style, bringing, among other effects, a generator which had been sold off cheap by the air force. Deadly serious hunters would never have tolerated the noise of a generator, supposing that it would scare away all the animals for miles around, but the Singhs rejoiced at having light in the evenings, and round the log fire they sang 'the songs of earlier days'. As Billy wrote, 'It was Balrampur all over again, except that the dramatis personae were different.'

One Christmas Billy went out with John Withnell, a friend of Balram's, and caught a young chital, which became a pet. Other creatures came to live with him, among them an eighteen-foot python, which he tethered with a rope collar until it developed a sore on its back and died; but in the end he decided that he had no right to take an animal from its environment and detain it for his pleasure.

Of far more practical use to him was an elephant named Bhagwan Piari (the Beloved of God), who came to him in the early 1950s, when the system of feudal rulers was abolished and the State of Balrampur had to disperse its elephant stable. A fine-looking creature, nine feet tall, she was said to be forty-five years old, and walked the 100-odd miles from her former home, taking four or five days. She and her new owner developed a strong mutual affection which (Billy reckoned) she demonstrated by urinating gallons whenever she saw him approaching.

She attended all the family's Christmas camps, and one of Billy's chief problems was to stop her filwan (keeper) Bhuntu from selling her special rations of unleavened wheat cakes (10 lbs a day) so that he could buy drink.

The elephant was a much steadier character, her worst weakness being a habit of wandering off down-river when Bhuntu took her for a bath – for she loved water, and often refused to come out. One of Billy's regrets was that he never learnt to drive Bhagwan Piari himself. (Later, in 1969, he acquired a second elephant, Sitara, or 'star', a nice-looking creature of about forty-five, who was sold off by one of the shikar companies when new legislation put them out of business.)

The holiday camps continued until 1962, but just after Christmas that year the family suffered another shattering blow. By then Jaswant had risen to become an Air Vice-

Marshal, and was Air Officer in Chief, Eastern Command. Because he always insisted on being actively employed, he had been flying helicopters on high-risk sorties in the war against China. In sharp contrast to other commanders, some of whom (including two major-generals, both winners of the Military Cross in World War II, and both former colleagues of his) had simply abandoned their posts and run away, he had been ferrying key people to and from the war zone in the mountainous border area which the Chinese had invaded, beyond the call of duty.

Clearly, he had been working under acute stress, and when on 31 December 1962 he joined the family for a New Year's dance at the Tollygunj Club in Calcutta – held to raise funds for women widowed during the campaign – he celebrated with his usual abandon, drinking a good deal. A few minutes after midnight, as the strains of *Auld Lang Syne* were dying away and the party was about to break up, he complained of a pain in his left arm, walked outside, apparently for a breath of fresh air, and collapsed on the putting green. Someone immediately summoned his big official car. Helpers loaded him into it and directed it to his house, where Billy and Balram heaved him up the stairs with his feet dragging. Until then nobody realized that he had had a fatal heart attack, but when their mother heard his feet bumping over the steps, she came out of her room and saw at once that he was dead. A doctor arrived at speed and plunged a needle into his chest, but it was too late: there was no flicker of response. Mabel sat watching as though she were made of stone, never uttering a sound.

After a post-mortem, a grand state funeral was held in Calcutta. High-ranking officers flew in from all over India, and in a moving ceremony at the cremation the senior commanders came up and saluted Mariam. As Billy wrote, 'We were devastated, for he was only forty-seven years old. Calcutta, the dirtiest and friendliest city in India, now lost all its charm for me.' Jaswant's family was left badly-off. The air force gave Mariam a small pension, but she had to find work, and eventually got a job with the British Council in Delhi.

~

People who met Billy in later life, when he was a confirmed bachelor, sometimes assumed that he had never been interested in girls – but this was far from true. The fact was that his chosen way of life, and place of domicile out in the wilds, had put him beyond the reach of any normal female company.

Earlier, things had been very different, and he pursued girls with enthusiasm. After various teenage crushes, at the end of his army service, he had an affair with Jean Thompson, sister of Henry Thompson, who ran a plywood business in Sitapur and a hide tannery in Kanpur. Jean had an excellent figure, but was at least three years older than him, and although he thought hard about marrying her, he could never bring himself to propose – partly, at least, because he feared she would turn him down.

Undaunted, he began courting Henry Thompson's daughter Juliette: as he put it, he 'sort of infested the family'. Juliette seemed a great catch: a fine-looking blonde, she held a private pilot's licence, had done eight parachute jumps, was intelligent and a great extrovert. Billy proposed to her 'perfunctorily', but she sidestepped – and perhaps it was just as well, for later she left a trail of havoc in her wake: she went to Australia, got married and divorced, then in East Africa married Graham Chubb, from whom she separated, set up with a South African, joined the rebels in Nigeria, fought a bull in Spain and taught in Saudi Arabia, before blazing back to

Australia, where she bought a house. (Later she often came to Tiger Haven, and once wrote to Mira saying, 'Tell Billy not to die before I see him again.') In spite of her many whirlwind affairs, she never had children.

Next came Razia, daughter of his childhood friend Minu's elder brother, who became ambassador to China. Razia was working as a journalist when Billy met her, but she went off and married a Lebanese.

More serious was Billy's courtship of Chandralekha, daughter of the distinguished politician Mrs Pandit, (sister of Jawaharlal Nehru, who was then Minister for Local Self-Government). Billy had met Mrs Pandit before he went overseas with the army, and he came across her again in Lucknow when his mother rented 98, The Mall. In the course of his search for a farm he looked at a property near Lucknow which had sullage (a process for distilling water) and as a sideline proposed to Chandralekha, a beautiful girl who had been to Wellesley College in America, and was then working as a journalist on the *Indian National Herald*.

His suit collapsed in less than romantic circumstances. He had taken her for a drive in a small Opel, and the car broke down, fortuitously right opposite the railway station at Bakhshi ka Talab, just outside Lucknow. When he proposed, as they sat in the front seats, Chandralekha tactfully pointed out that she was a career girl at heart – so they gloomily abandoned the dead vehicle and went back into the city by train.

More dangerous, and more thrilling, was his clandestine affair with Creina, the attractive Anglo-Indian wife of Jim Stephens, who had formed a farming partnership with Billy's landlord, George Hearsey. The Stephens lived in a thatched cottage, a lovely old house built on English lines, in Pallia: Jim drank a good deal, and talked incessantly, droning on at such

length that Billy's mother once put her sari over her head, as if
to shield herself from the sun, and went to sleep inside it while
he continued his monologue. He was very unkind to Creina,
and she, being thirty-two years younger, used to rove around.
Billy felt fairly sure that Jim knew about his involvement, but
although it was exciting, it came to nothing. By then he had
decided that he did not want to live permanently with any
woman, and he was afraid of getting trapped. He realized that
he had greater empathy with animals than with humans, and
in any case he was driven by his desire to get things done.

~

In 1955 he at last started to build himself a permanent house
at Jasbirnagar, a concrete structure in which, at first, he
omitted to install any windows. Only when his mother
remonstrated did he punch some holes in the walls; and now
that he had a dwelling which other human beings considered
habitable, Mabel often came to stay. Yet he himself was
altogether in a disturbed state. After nine years in a straw hut,
he found he derived no pleasure from living in a more
substantial building, and at the same time his feelings about
wildlife 'were at a stage of ambivalence'.

Killing no longer gave him any sense of achievement: the
slaughter of a wolf that had taken one of his goats brought him
no satisfaction.

His moment of truth occurred in 1960, when Balram came
out from Calcutta, and the pair of them went for a drive in the
forest. After dark had fallen, they sat down for a cup of tea
beside a log fire – and the rest of the story is best told in Billy's
own words:

> A lapwing called across a depression, and soon after a leopard
> gave a succession of sawing grunts. He was objecting to the

invasion of his territory. I drove my jeep to the edge of the depression and saw in the glow of the headlights a lambent green pinpoint of light moving at right angles to our front.

Resting my elbows on my knees, I took careful aim at the moving pinpoint, and fired a shot. There was no sound, but the light went out. I advanced to the spot, and in the flashlight saw a leopard lying on the ground. A crimson circle welled behind the shoulder and, even as I watched, the fire faded from his eyes. I had brought off a spectacular shot and acquired a fine trophy, but I felt nothing but an awful confusion – futility at the destruction of beauty and the taking of life for personal pleasure. I put aside my rifle, as my father had done many years before.

This, he later came to realize, was a turning-point in his life – the moment at which his true conversion began.

Apart from guilt, his worst anxiety was the spread of cultivation. More and more farmers kept arriving in the area, many of them dispossessed people from Pakistan, and as they eroded the grassland, the once-teeming wildlife – the nilgai, the blackbuck, the barasingha and the chital – dwindled and withdrew. The process was accelerated by a government colonization scheme, designed to settle landless labourers from eastern Uttar Pradesh, who took over large tracts of Majhra Singahi, Vizzy's old hunting-ground.

All at once Billy felt that he had been 'smothered by cultivation', and that he must find some other land, further from human occupation. He had heard of one possible area, called Billahia, about five miles due north of Jasbirnagar, just outside the southern edge of the Dudhwa Reserved Forest, which was known mainly as a place where poachers went to shoot animals or steal firewood. The ground had been leased by a politician who thought he could make money by extracting timber from the jungle, so that for him the land's immediate proximity to the forest was an advantage. Luckily he had been inhibited by the fact that a small river called the Neora ran east and west along the foot of the escarpment which formed the forest's southern boundary, effectively cutting it off from the south. Another problem was that the grasslands through which he would have to extract the timber were waterlogged for half the year, during and after the monsoon. In spite of these handicaps, he had made a start, and a ford known as Chorleek (Robbers' Path), which led from the grassland into the forest, had become well-used.

One morning in 1959 Billy set off on Bhagwan Piari to assess the land for himself, accompanied by his big brown mongrel Pincha, then about four years old. When they crossed a bhagar – a low-lying, marshy watercourse – the elephant forged straight ahead, but the dog sometimes had to swim, biting his way through the reeds. On higher ground he made better going as he followed the channels which the five-ton pachyderm trampled through the grass. In the distance ahead the forest on the escarpment loomed like a vast green curtain drawn across the horizon.

The first stream the party reached was the Soheli, a tributary of the Neora, winding in from the south-west, and above it they saw a large python coiled in a tree. On their right, parallel with the river, lay a lake known as Tela Tal. Duck rose from its surface, and flights of green parrots came screeching overhead, on the way from the jungle to their feeding-grounds. Then the explorers reached a point where the two rivers flowed together. At the junction, pale green water swirled in a pool about thirty yards across and fifty long. Emerald kingfishers flashed across it. On the near side, where they stood on slightly higher land, the air was loud with the buzz of insects. At their feet the current flowed through the pool from left to right, opaque with silt washed down from the hills of Nepal.

Within a few yards of the far shore, opposite them to the north, rose the escarpment, a bank of earth and rock some fifty feet high, following the line of the river, east and west. On the top of the escarpment soared the majestic sal, their trunks rising a hundred feet or more, as straight as columns in some arboreal cathedral. Fifty miles further to the north, sparkling in the clear morning light, tier upon tier of mountains massed towards the eternal snows of Nanda Devi and Dhaulagiri, visible through gaps in the forest.

Billy was enchanted by the setting – the meeting of the waters, the jungle immediately beyond, the abundance of birds (orioles, drongos, mynahs, bulbuls), the absence of human activity, the Himalayan peaks on the horizon. Here, he thought, was 'the last bastion' in his retreat from manmade settlements. Here he would build his lasting home. Here he would live in harmony with the forest and its creatures. To him, the call of the wild was irresistible.

It seems ironic that once again his aim was to farm – to tame part of the wilderness on which his spiritual well-being depended, and to remove some of the fine, isolated trees that rose out of the grass. Yet that was what he planned to do. Having rented 173 acres of scrub-land, he started to clear them, using a combination of elephant and tractor-power to dig out the roots of scattered jamun and silk-cotton trees and drag them away. As the plough bit into the virgin soil, it cut through dozens of snakes which had been living just underground, and left their sliced-up bodies writhing amid the upturned earth. He collected a gang of about ten men to work with him, and as he recalled later, they felt extraordinarily isolated, cut off from contact with the outside world. A well

provided them with water, and they supplemented their
normal rations with the meat of the occasional wild pig or deer,
shot in the fields.

Although a road of sorts passed the property about a mile
to the east, running north and south, there was not even a
track leading to the site, and at first the only access on foot was
by means of a tree that had fallen across the river. Later he had
a rough approach-road constructed, but for the time being
everything had to be brought in by elephant or crawler tractor.

Once more he built himself a straw hut in which to live. At
first he decided to call the place Dream Farm, because he
thought the soil must have been richly fertilized by silt spilling
out of the river during the monsoon floods; but later he
changed the name to Tiger Haven, partly in memory of
Jaswant, partly because he hoped the place would become a
haven for the great carnivores.

As he soon realized, the area suffered from one major
disadvantage: during the monsoon, from June to August, and
for weeks afterwards, the land was intermittently under water
– partly because the meandering Soheli was choked with fallen
trees, but mainly because, a mile to the east, the flow of the
river was constricted by an embankment which carried the
railway.

When the line was built in 1920, the engineers had made
the spans of the bridge over the river too small to
accommodate the huge amount of water coming down after
monsoon rains – and the problem was exacerbated later when
the road to the north was metalled, following the line of the
railway, and the engineer in charge reduced the number of
bridge-spans from three to two, in a deliberate act of revenge
after he had been caught poaching. During the monsoon
floods Billy's chosen site was often completely cut off by water,

and to reach it he either had to walk a mile and a half along the escarpment from the settlement of Dudhwa and cross the swollen river by boat, or come in on the elephant. Each flood generally subsided within a day or so, but access remained uncertain during the rainy season.

Living alongside the jungle, he was far closer to its creatures than he had been at Jasbirnagar, and so that he could observe them more easily, he built a little summer-house around a jamun tree on the bank of the Junction Pool. The river was full of fish and turtles, marsh crocodiles and gangetic dolphins. Chital deer often walked by along the opposite bank; occasionally a bear came foraging, or a leopard padded silently past. Commonest of all were the monkeys – the small, brown rhesus monkeys, and the larger, white-coated, black-faced langurs, which used their long, curved tails for balance. On the cleared land south of the river, peacocks paraded, and jungle fowl scuttled. Only the tigers remained out of sight, although pug marks showed that they were active at night; and whenever some predator went on the move during daylight hours, its progress would be heralded by a cacophony of alarm calls – urgent honks from peacocks, the coughs of monkeys, the barking of muntjac and the piping whistles of hog deer.

Within a year of moving north, Billy began to construct more permanent dwellings. His first building was a prefabricated house made of jacksboard – a kind of plywood – and it was inhabited by his mother when she came to stay. Next, using bricks baked from clay in primitive kilns close at hand, he started on a house proper. At first the building was single-storey, but later he added a second storey to parts of it. Bit by bit he extended the dwelling, until a line of low, white buildings, set in a slight curve, stretched for nearly a hundred yards along the bank of the river – and in 1972, when he was hoping for a visit from Mrs Indira Gandhi, the Prime Minister, he added a spacious upstairs room for her to occupy, exactly as, during the sixteenth century, the owners of grand country houses in England built on an extra wing when a visit from Queen Elizabeth I was in the offing.

Gradually he settled into a regular pattern of activity. For eight months of the year he lived at Tiger Haven, running in the cool of the early morning, working-out with his weights, and labouring on the farm land with his men. Then, towards the end of June, the call of the pied-crested cuckoo would warn him with unfailing accuracy that the onset of the monsoon was imminent, and as the first showers swept in, he would pack his belongings into a trailer and drive down to Jasbirnagar, which he still owned.

At Tiger Haven, manned only by some of his staff, the flood waters would rise and fall, rise and fall, sometimes invading the house to a depth of two feet or more, so that all the books, pictures and furniture had to be moved upstairs. In October the appearance of another bird, the redstart, heralded the return of cool, clear weather, and he would eagerly head north again to resume his station on the edge of the jungle.

With its whitewashed walls and cement floors, Tiger Haven was never luxuriously furnished, and in the early days the only electricity was provided by a generator; but the presence of a small army of servants to cook, hew firewood, heat the bath water, wash clothes, wait at table and feed the animals meant that family and friends could come and stay in comfort. Billy designed the bedrooms so that each had a bathroom to which the staff could gain access by way of steep steps at the back, and anyone who wanted a candle-lit bath would find his (or her) tin tub filled with scalding water, with a couple more steaming buckets set beside it. Excellent food, and roaring log fires on chilly winter evenings, made a stay at Tiger Haven highly enjoyable. Later, Billy had a fireplace built in the sitting-room, but in the early days everyone sat round blazing logs in a pit outside, with the sweet scent of jamun wood smoke drifting in the night air. Billy was scrupulous about not cutting down live trees for firewood, and always collected fallen timber from the forest.

Surrounded as he was by the wealth of wildlife, he was drawn more and more into the struggle to save it; and because the officials of the forest division were so ineffective, he increasingly took matters into his own hands. His main concern in the early days was a huge herd of barasingha or swamp deer which lived in a 3,000-acre bowl of marshy grassland, with a lake in the middle, in an area called Ghola, some five miles west of Tiger Haven. This was recognized as one of the swamp deer's last major refuges in the whole of India, and the official estimate of the herd's total was 1,500.

Because the Central Government was planning to impose a ceiling on all land holdings, and limit the number of acres any individual might farm, Billy saw that this wonderful natural habitat would inevitably be broken up and leased to small-time cultivators. Therefore, when the State Board of Wildlife for Uttar Pradesh was formed in 1964, and he was appointed a member, he submitted a resolution calling for the entire 3,000 acres to be made part of the North Kheri Reserved Forest, and thus saved from any form of exploitation.

The chief wildlife warden came down from Lucknow, and after Billy had taken him on a tour of the Ghola lake, he went away making firm promises that something would be done. Yet for a year nothing happened, and when land-grabbers began to appear on the scene, Billy himself went into action. First, under strong protest from local forest staff, he ploughed up some land within the forest boundary, planted it with barley and furnished it with salt licks, to provide attractive feeding areas for the swamp deer. Then, as soon as the barley was sprouting, he borrowed five elephants from a shikar company to reinforce Bhagwan Piari and organized a huge drive, to push the deer towards the forest. Some broke back, but the main herd, estimated at 600 head, crossed the Soheli and entered the protected area.

With him that day was the distinguished American naturalist George Schaller, who, although only in his thirties, had already studied mountain gorillas in Africa and now was spending a year living among tigers in the Kanha National Park, in Madhya Pradesh. Another of his interests was the swamp deer, and his outing with Billy made an indelible impression, which he recorded in his diary:

> 27 February 1965. With typical hospitality Billy has invited me to stay at his farm. He rises at dawn and lifts weights on the verandah. He seems a bit shy about this as I watch him, but I admire his strength and determination. On one side of his home is the sluggish Soheli river and beyond it the forest; on the other side his acres of sugar cane, now being harvested, and swampy meadows ...
>
> Billy throws rice to the wild jungle fowl which come from nearby thickets. A distant chital deer gives an alarm bell: perhaps a tiger is on the move. At 8.30 we have tea.
>
> He has one elephant, and borrows five others from a neighbour. Spread out in a line, the elephants glide through the marsh. A thin line of trees marks the hazy horizon. Grass swishes against my elephant's body, and its feet splash in the stagnant water. The only human sound is the occasional command of a mahout urging his elephant on. The whole scene is an evocation of the past, of India a hundred years ago ...
>
> The elephants flush a few deer, mostly the small hog deer. But suddenly a brown wave of swamp deer tightly bunched

churns and crashes away. It thunders on, splitting and rejoining, until it disappears. I cannot count the animals, but estimate 500 to 600.

Billy has given me a wonderful present: a marvellous and unique wildlife experience. I fervently hope that he can somehow protect this fragment of India's natural heritage. Later we sit by a bonfire and drink tea, wholly content, the shared experience and joy in nature forming a strong bond of companionship.

Billy, for his part, enormously admired the dedication with which Schaller conducted his research, and feared he would never be able to emulate the American, in either patience or efficiency.

Although the drive had not turned out anything like the official total of 1,500 deer, next day Billy was delighted to count 450 grazing in the meadow at Sathiana, one of the forest rest houses. So far, so good. But the deer were outnumbered by domestic cattle, whose owners paid the forest department a small subsidy, and Billy was determined to get rid of these alien grazers. With the cooperation of a sympathetic divisional forest officer, he resorted to strong-arm tactics, setting fire to the graziers' huts and hitching one recalcitrant fellow by a rope to the towing-hook of his jeep. As he drove slowly down the forest road, he was pursued by 'a strange assortment of sounds coming from the rear'. The graziers came to realize that his formidable physique was matched by steely determination, and soon, as he put it, 'the barasingha were in and the cattle out'.

Still the deer needed protection, for poachers kept sneaking in, and graziers kept infiltrating. Billy himself patrolled the forest day and night, and in the intervals lobbied ceaselessly on the barasinghas' behalf, submitting papers to the Wildlife Board, and making the tedious six-hour journey to their meetings in Lucknow.

Just as he was beginning to despair, help arrived in the form of a new state forest minister, Charan Singh, who had a genuine interest in wildlife. Swayed by Billy's arguments, he announced that an area of eighty-two square miles – some 55,000 acres – surrounding Tiger Haven on the north side, would be declared a wildlife sanctuary.

The news gave Billy a huge surge of hope. He had asked for a reserve of forty square miles, and suddenly he had double that. The sanctuary, to be called Dudhwa, stretched twenty-five miles from east to west, half on each side of Tiger Haven, and reaching three miles into the forest towards the Nepal border. About a quarter of it was open grassland, where the swamp deer could graze, and the rest was forest.

~

Once Billy had more or less given up shooting with guns, he took enthusiastically to shooting with film, and in 1965 the acquisition of a 35 mm camera, together with a telephoto lens, persuaded him to lay aside firearms altogether, except in emergencies. He had conceived a great admiration for Fred Champion who had really pioneered tiger photography between the World Wars. His early results were encouraging, but his physical clumsiness was always a handicap, and he never attained the proficiency for which he hoped. Even when he bought more sophisticated equipment – flash guns and triggering devices – his pictures often proved disappointing, especially when he tried to identify individual tigers by photographing them at night, and absolute precision of focus became essential.

For years the barasingha remained of high interest to him. Again and again in the winter he would walk out from Tiger Haven to their grazing grounds, followed by Bhagwan Piari and her mahout. At the edge of the open area the team would split, the elephant continuing along the edge of the forest to the south, and he making for a machan perched in an isolated tree near the centre of the grassland. There he would wait, with a grand view of the Himalayas to the north, while the elephant approached in wide sweeps from the opposite direction, moving (as he put it) 'like some great ocean liner on the horizon', pushing the deer a little further towards him with each advance. Often herds would end up almost under him, oblivious of his presence, enabling him to observe their behaviour closely.

Before the start of the annual rut, in early September, the swamp deer naturally segregate into different sexes, hinds in big groups, stags in others. Barasingha means 'twelve horns' or points, and with their long, many-tined antlers the massed stags made a memorable sight, like a regiment of soldiers armed with spears. The onset of the rut was always signalled by the calls of the master-stags known as 'bugling', which Billy described as sounding like 'hon-HON, hon-HON, hon-HON, repeated about a dozen times, with the second note drawn out and gradually fading away, while a curious metallic drone continues in the background.' The sound, he wrote, was 'dramatic enough for all conversation at the campfire to cease for the period of its duration.'

Study of the swamp deer was his first detailed observation of wildlife. Yet by 1969 the main focus of his attention was being drawn to the great predators, the leopards and tigers, whose numbers were dwindling even faster than those of the ungulates. The more he studied them, the more their independent habits and solitary nature appealed to him, and the more determined he became to do something for their cause.

When he first arrived at Tiger Haven, there were three resident leopards in the immediate neighbourhood, but within a few years they were dead, and the population as a whole had been whittled away by poachers shooting the cats for their skins, then still a valuable commodity. By the time the ban on the sale of skins came into force, there was scarcely a leopard left in the whole of the Dudhwa area.

Tigers were surviving better, but they too were in mortal danger, for although officially protected, they were bitterly hated by the villagers whose cattle and buffaloes they took, and they were being shot or blown up with primitive bombs by anyone who dared to take them on. Besides, the enmity of ordinary people was — and is — compounded by the way in which the forests were organized. Then, as now, animals lived in the forests, and the forests were controlled ultimately by politicians, who depended for their votes on men who detested the great cats and constantly demanded their extermination.

By 1969, concern had spread to national and international level. In November that year, at the general assembly of the International Union for the Conservation of Nature (IUCN), held in Delhi, a paper by Kailash Sankhala stressed the severity of the tigers' decline. A nation-wide census had suggested that, in contrast with a population of perhaps 40,000 between the two World Wars, there were only 1,827 left in the whole of India, and at the end of the deliberations Billy proposed a ban on all tiger-shooting. The assembly passed a resolution proposing a moratorium on hunting, and suggested that the income earned by shikar companies in the past should be replaced by straightforward tourism. The resolution swiftly put paid to twenty-six hunting firms, which were too hidebound to transfer their activities into tourism, and went out of business.

The next major advance came in 1970 at a joint meeting of

the IUCN and the World Wildlife Fund in Switzerland, at which the British naturalist Guy Mountfort (a trustee of the WWF) was authorized to offer India one million dollars to launch an all-out effort to save the tiger from extinction. The Indian prime minister, Mrs Indira Gandhi, who had a strong personal interest in wildlife, reacted with alacrity. A task force was appointed and initially identified nine project areas, and a special committee to initiate action was setup, headed by Dr Karan Singh (son of the Maharaja of Kashmir), the Minister for Tourism and Chairman of the Indian Board for Wildlife.

From day one the project was seriously hampered by the fact that it had been placed under the control of the forest department. Interested international bodies all emphasized the earning potential of wildlife tourism, as demonstrated in Africa, and urged that the tiger scheme should come under the Ministry of Tourism. But India stuck to its old ways and kept wildlife lumped in with forestry. Had Mrs Gandhi followed through and taken Billy's advice to separate forestry and wildlife management, the tigers' chances would have been immeasurably improved; but the status quo remained.

In Billy's eyes this was a disaster, and in September 1971, when Mrs Gandhi called a meeting of senior figures, both official and otherwise, connected with wildlife, he said so in no muffled terms. Normally he is not very articulate, but on that occasion anger gave wings to his words. Dr M.K. Ranjitsinh, a senior civil servant, recalls:

> The meeting ended with a tirade by Billy against the prime minister and her government. "What priority does wildlife have in your scheme of things, Madam Prime Minister?" he asked in his stentorian voice, and then arrayed before her the plight of wildlife in India, and of his beloved Dudhwa in particular. Mrs Gandhi flinched, became defensive, even pensive.

On many occasions Billy pointed out that forestry and wildlife are mutually antagonistic, 'and cannot be meaningfully managed by the same facility'. A forester's aim is always to make money by selling trees for timber – but tree-felling amounts to destruction of habitat, and cannot be permitted in areas reserved for wildlife. The forest department was naturally loath to allocate further areas to wildlife, as any such change would bring commercial activities to an end and reduce revenue.

Notwithstanding these anomalies, in 1972 the government passed the Indian Wildlife Act, which at last set realistic schedules and penalties, and in September that year the World Wildlife Fund launched Operation Tiger, a global fund-raising scheme. So firmly did this catch people's imagination that 1.8 million dollars were contributed in a single year, much of the money coming from schoolchildren. Project Tiger was officially inaugurated at the Corbett National Park in April 1973, and India adopted the tiger as its national animal. Like everyone else concerned, Billy hoped that, against all the odds, the project would succeed; but in the meanwhile he had begun hatching a major conservation scheme of his own.

FIVE

EELIE AND PRINCE

The year 1971 brought two new arrivals to Tiger Haven. The first was a dog, the second a leopard, and both had a profound effect on Billy's life.

Early one morning in October he was sitting out on the bank of the Junction Pool with a cup of tea, as was his wont, when he saw a gang of labourers approaching, on their way to repair earth roads washed out by the monsoon floods. They were led by a forest guard in khaki uniform, and behind them trotted a forlorn little, sandy-coloured creature which looked at first glance like a jackal – except that its thick tail stood upright and curled over at the top.

The forest guard, an old friend, paused for a chat before continuing on his way. Then he and his men trudged off into the trees. Glancing after them, Billy realized that something was missing from the picture, and when he turned back, he saw that the dog had stayed behind. She looked about six months old, and, like most Indian strays, was thoroughly malnourished. There she sat, miserably thin, with ribs and hip bones showing through her skin, and when she moved, she walked with a slight limp. But out of her pert and perky face shone a pair of lustrous eyes, rimmed with black, and from the way she confidentially accepted a piece of toast, Billy knew she had come to stay.

His mother Mabel, who was in residence at the time, could not believe he would want another dog so soon after losing both his earlier canine companions. The first to go had been Susie, a black Labrador given to him twelve years earlier by the wife of a policeman in Nainital. Yet the one he really mourned was his mongrel Pincha, whom he had for sixteen years, and who had recently been found dead on the edge of the Neora, having rolled down the bank into the water.

Mabel herself loved dogs, but after the recent traumas she could not bear the thought of more canine crises, and she therefore told the servants to drive the vagrant away. They duly bombarded the little bitch with sticks and lumps of earth, but she dodged the missiles easily enough and hung around. The person who saved her was Billy's nephew Jairaj, (Jaswant and Mariam's son, known as Tiggy), who was working at Jasbirnagar. With his grandmother still objecting, and warning, 'You'll never get rid of it if you feed it,' he found the bitch something to eat.

Closer inspection revealed that she was suffering from some virulent form of mange, which Jairaj cured with remedies from the local vet. Soon the little dog had become everyone's favourite, and Billy named her Eelie, because the extravagant, hooped bend of her tail reminded him of an eel.

Mabel's prophecy – 'You'll never get rid of it' – was borne out a hundred times over. To say that Eelie became Billy's most faithful companion would hardly do her justice. For thirteen years she was his closest confederate, his inseparable companion, a partner who joined in his jungle patrols with evident enjoyment and, at home, created a unique bridge between the domestic world of man and the wild world of tigers, leopards and lesser creatures. Her most astonishing achievement was to dominate three leopards and a tiger, even when they had grown to several times her weight and size, and her character in many ways matched that of her master. Like him, she was fearless, tough and intelligent, and affectionate without ever being demonstrative. Like him, she loved the jungle and was fascinated by its inhabitants.

Walking in the forest with her new master was by no means free of risk, for he never carried any weapon except for a stick. Leopards eat dogs with relish, often snatching them from villages, and Eelie could easily have been grabbed by a leopard or a tiger when she and her mentor were moving through thick cover. Yet she quickly showed that she had a strong instinct for self-preservation, and weighed up her new environment with remarkable speed, concentrating intently as she assessed the scent patterns left by animals that had moved around in the night.

She would sniff the places where a tiger had scraped the ground or sprayed urine on a tree trunk to mark its territory, and linger over the excavations of wild pigs. Even without a mother to teach her, she knew that it was safe to chase chital, but that any sign of a leopard or tiger demanded intense caution.

As for Bhagwan Piari and Sitara, she treated them as coolly as if she had lived with elephants all her life, even trying to steal Sitara's roti from under the tip of her trunk – a habit that alarmed Billy, because he knew that if the elephant merely put its foot on her, that would be the end. When the household moved to Jasbirnagar for the next monsoon, in June 1972, she quickly settled down in amity with Sister Guptara and Elizabeth Taylor, the two rhesus monkeys which lived there.

Monkeys were one hazard for a young dog to contend with, a leopard something else – and when Billy was offered a cub, he knew that to adopt it would be a tricky undertaking. Yet for some time he had been wondering if it would be possible to bolster the population of wild carnivores by rearing one and releasing it into the jungle, and when the chance came, he jumped at it.

The male cub he acquired was an orphan, picked up in Bihar after his mother had been killed, and reared by Anne Wright, a well-known conservationist who lived in Calcutta, and her daughter Belinda, known as 'Blue'. Since the Wrights had already brought up a tiger and a lion, they were familiar with big cats, and reckoned the leopard their most entertaining cub of all. But by the time he was three months old, he was over two feet long, weighed 30 lbs, moved like lightning and had become altogether too much of a handful for people living in a city, even though they had a sizeable compound. Anne therefore offered him to Billy.

The journey from Calcutta to Jasbirnagar went remarkably well. Keeping the cub on a lead, Anne and her daughter Belinda booked a first-class compartment on the overnight train to Lucknow, where Billy met the party with his jeep, and they all spent the next night at Sitapur, with his friends Henry and Sue Thomson. The leopard slept in the same room as his two female minders, and during the next day's drive sat calmly in the back of the vehicle – until an unwary wayfarer tried to thumb a lift and started climbing aboard before anyone could warn him that the only spare seat had already been taken by an unusual passenger. When the leopard dug its claws into his arm, he leapt off as if electrocuted.

Billy was naturally nervous about how Eelie would react to the spotted newcomer. At first she was hostile, and growled at the leopard whenever he approached her, laying back her ears and trying to nip him. Gradually the sparring subsided, and they settled down to an amicable co-existence.

Having no guidance in how to handle a leopard, Billy had to experiment from day to day. The cub was quite destructive, ripping up blankets and knocking down plates, and Billy banned him from the house. At night he anchored him with a leather collar and lead on the verandah, where he slept on a pile of straw alongside his new master's bed, with Eelie curled up on the other side.

Anne had called the cub Cheetla, the local word for leopard, but Billy called him Prince, because he regarded the leopard as the prince of cats. To help look after him, he took on a boy named Munna, but after only a month he became frightened and left. His replacement, twenty-year-old Ganga Ram, had already been working for Billy as a farmhand and adapted well, establishing a good relationship with his charge.

When they moved up to Tiger Haven for the winter, Eelie sat in the passenger seat of the jeep, and Prince rode behind. The roundabout journey – some ten miles in all, first to the east, then to the north and back to the west – went smoothly, and that night Billy slept out on the verandah with one animal on either side of his bed. In the morning, to his dismay, he found that Eelie had vanished. When searches failed to discover her, he could only conclude that she had made her way back to Jasbirnagar – and so she had, somehow navigating her way across five miles of open country.

Her tracks showed that she had taken a direct route, and Billy was astonished, for her feat confirmed to him what he had seen many times already – that animals have powers of direction-finding denied to humans. It made him realize how much of their original instincts human beings have lost through the development of speech and thought.

Billy had expected that Prince would instinctively feel at home in the forest, but he found exactly the opposite. The cub would not go into the jungle, which seemed to strike him as a hostile environment, and he much preferred the sunny, open farmland. Although sometimes restrained by a collar and lead at night, he was never kept in a cage during the day, but was left loose to wander about the house and its surroundings as he liked.

Remembering how Joy Adamson's lioness Elsa loved playing with a motor tyre suspended on a rope, Billy fixed one up for Prince – but the young leopard had no time for it. His chief recreation was climbing trees, at which he was phenomenally agile. Although he often lay on branches, he had no need of any when climbing or descending: he would hurtle straight up smooth trunks, stop half-way, hanging on with his claws, then turn and come down again, all with apparently effortless ease.

He also spent countless hours playing with Eelie. The bitch was then about eighteen months old, at the height of her youthful vigour, and the energy which the two expended was amazing. Around the house they continually stalked, ambushed, charged and jumped on each other, and down by the river they raced in circles over the sandy spits and through the shallows. Billy, watching them with delight, realized that for the leopard all this was unconscious preparation for the serious business of catching and killing prey, on which he would depend for his survival; but it was also clear that in all the games Eelie was dominant. Even when Prince grew to more than double her size and weight, she still controlled proceedings, and would stop them with a nip or a growl when she had had enough. Whenever a wrestle ended with the leopard sitting on top of her, he would gaze into the distance as though trying to take his mind off the fact that a juicy snack was trapped beneath him.

High among his amusements was the destruction of Billy's property. He tore a mattress to shreds, ripped up Eelie's bedding, disembowelled an eiderdown, exploded a pillow and shredded an overcoat, before sneaking into Billy's dressing-room, where he punched a hole in a tube of shaving cream and broke a bottle of after-shave lotion. Billy, incensed, grabbed him by the scuff of the neck and threw him out – and then was agreeably surprised to find that Prince bore him no resentment, but immediately came and rubbed against him with his normal friendliness.

One night, as leopard, man and dog prepared to sleep side by side on the verandah, Billy noticed that Prince was sitting upright, apparently watching something close to him, and when he switched on his torch, the beam picked out the yellow-and-black markings of a banded krait, sliding past a few inches away. The leopard seemed quite unworried, but Billy, knowing that the five-foot snake harboured venom sixteen times as poisonous as that of a cobra, grabbed a stick and whacked it across the back of the head. The blow disabled it and left it writhing round in a semicircle, so that he was able to finish it off with a few more hits on the head.

Billy deliberately made no attempt to domesticate the cub or to correct his behaviour. The result was that the leopard never acquired any sense of right and wrong – as a dog does with training – and in consequence was always a threat to small children, which he looked on as monkeys, and therefore as potential prey. Billy first became aware of the danger when Prince, at about eight months, attacked and scratched two young daughters of labourers working on the farm. Neither girl was seriously hurt, but the incident forced Billy to two conclusions. One was that he must move the leopard away from Tiger Haven to a base deeper in the forest, and the other that in future animals and birds must have priority at the farm: henceforth, agriculture would be confined to the production of crops for wildlife, mainly deer, and his staff of eight or ten men were forbidden to bring any children with them when they came to work.

Thus Prince precipitated a fundamental change. Yet the labourers were by no means the only people nervous of the adolescent carnivore. Billy's mother, being very small and light, was also scared of the animal, so he converted the hut round the jamun tree by the Junction Pool into an airy enclosure, with walls of wire netting and a pointed roof of thatch. The structure became known as 'Gran's Cage' and in it Mabel would sit knitting, reading, doing the *Statesman* crossword or playing Scrabble while Prince wandered around outside. Occasionally she would sigh and say, 'What kind of a life is this?' and then in an Urdu expression, 'Everything's ulta pulta – upside-down!' On the whole, though, she was content to feel safe. Sometimes Eelie spent time with her inside the cage, but more often she acted as the frail old lady's bodyguard in the open, escorting her about and seeing off Prince if he tried to harass her. In the evenings Mabel enjoyed a stiff peg of Gordons' gin, which Jim Stevens used to procure for her.

One day the gang of walkers went off as usual on their morning reconnaissance – Billy, Prince, Eelie and Ganga Ram. Granny was ensconced in her cage when suddenly, to her horror, she saw Prince returning prematurely on his own, creeping towards her, belly to the ground. For a few seconds she sat rigidly poised on a blue cushion in her cane chair.

Four Musketeers: (left to right) baby Balram,
eldest brother Jaswant, Billy and sister Amar

♦♦♦

(*Family photos: Courtesy Brinda Dubey*)

Grand matriarch: Billy's mother Mabel at her home in Lucknow

Facing page: (above) Family portrait, 1957 - Mabel and Billy flank
the rest of the family; (below) Hunter turned conservationist -
Billy at 14 with his first tiger kill in Balrampur

♦♦♦

(Family photos: Courtesy Brinda Dubey)

No crocodile tears: Billy with a baby croc (*Photo: Ashish Chandola*)

Facing page: Billy (on tree) with Jaswant; the two brothers with a friend at Pallia; Billy and Balram flank future Air Marshall Jaswant Singh

◆◆◆

(*Family photos: Courtesy Brinda Dubey*)

Leopard games: Prince, Billy's first Big Cat, mock-charging at Tiger Haven, and (facing page) Billy demonstrating his weigh-lifting abilities with a young Harriet.

✦✦✦

(*Photos: Courtesy Billy Arjan Singh*)

Billy in an expansive mood relaxing on the verandah of Tiger Haven

♦♦♦

(*Photo: Sarah Giles*)

Then, as the leopard lunged at the door and burst it open, she closed her eyes and dropped her hands, giving herself up for lost. The next thing she knew, Prince was sitting beside her, licking her hand.

To Amar, he seemed a jovial creature, with a definite sense of humour; but when her daughter Priya was nine or ten, and lightly built, she became nervous of him, because he would come up on her from behind with a swift and silent rush, and put his paws on her hips. He never clawed or scratched her, but his motives remained enigmatic, and Priya could not feel safe with him about.

To furnish the leopard with a forest base was relatively simple. At a point about a mile west of Tiger Haven, Billy supervised the construction of a large machan, supported on four living jamun trees, and equipped with a sloping ladder for easy access. When he first took Prince there, the leopard shot straight up one of the trees, ignoring the ladder; and, once up, refused to come down. Without Billy's reassuring presence, he did not feel secure enough to move around the jungle on his own, and for several days he remained aloft, descending only to eat the meals brought out to him and go for accompanied walks.

In an attempt to supplement his diet with roughage, Billy took to shooting the odd parrot or dove with his .22 rifle, but Prince frustrated the attempts to feed him feathers by carefully plucking each bird before he ate it. He and Eelie soon learnt to associate the crack of the rifle with the thud of a bird falling, and both would bound in the direction of the noise. If the bitch reached the spot first, she would drive the leopard off the kill, but if he won the race, he would take the offering straight up a tree, thus putting an end to any dispute. If Billy kept missing – as he often did – Prince would sometimes jump on him as if to say, 'What the hell are you up to?'

With or without roughage, he was always extremely clean, and the number of his own hairs in his droppings bore witness to the many hours of grooming he put in. Gradually he began to kill for himself, mainly chital fawns and monkeys, and he became increasingly independent. Yet whenever he was in earshot he would respond to Billy's call and run to meet him, passing between his straddled legs and rubbing against him. Billy would then lead off for a walk, and afterwards both would sit together on the sand by the river for ten minutes or more, often in physical contact, which the leopard clearly enjoyed. Sometimes Prince would doze, but whenever he was awake, his eyes, ears and nose were continually on the alert, twitching to pick up messages from the jungle, and Billy realized that his sight and hearing were far sharper than those of humans.

Prince was nearly a year old when he began to squirt: spray a jet of urine, or urine mixed with a secretion from the anal glands, on to bushes, logs and tree trunks along the trail. The habit is vital to the survival of both leopards and tigers, for volatile, heavily-armed predators need to avoid each other as much as possible, and squirting announces an animal's presence, either attracting members of the opposite sex, or warning those of the same sex to keep their distance.

Prince faced numerous threats, the most persistent being that from a young tigress, which began to frequent the area of his machan, perhaps attracted by his squirting. Then Billy came across a party of ten men, one of whom had a gun, crossing the river near Leopard Haven (as Prince's treetop perch came to be called). When he challenged them, they bolted, amid volleys of abuse, but he felt sure they had been after Prince, as the Nepal border was very close, and once across it they could easily have sold his skin for a good price.

The greatest menace, however, came from the weather. Billy knew that when the monsoon broke, the dirt road between the farm and Leopard Haven would be cut off. To safeguard Prince during the wet weather, he built yet another tree platform, this time on the escarpment north of the river, so high above river level that there was no chance of it being flooded. He called this the Monsoon Machan, and during the rains it served its purpose well, its drawback being that the approach to it – by jeep, bicycle and on foot – was long and difficult.

With the onset of the rains, Billy once again decamped to Jasbirnagar, taking Eelie with him, and when he came back every second day, bringing meat for Prince, he left the dog behind. The result was that for several months the leopard did not see his companion, and the separation led to a revealing incident.

When the floods receded, Eelie was pregnant for the second time, so Billy left her at Jasbirnagar and, instead, brought a son from her first litter to Tiger Haven. The dog looked so exactly like her that most people could not distinguish between the two, but the moment Prince saw (or possibly smelt) him, he launched an attack, clearly bent on killing and eating him. Only the dog's speed saved his life – and the incident proved to Billy even more clearly that Prince knew Eelie not as a dog but as an individual. When the two were reunited, they resumed their relationship as if it had never been interrupted.

During walks the leopard still behaved like a boisterous schoolboy, charging through undergrowth, rushing up trees and leaping onto Billy's shoulders. Occasionally he knocked his mentor down and sat on his legs, and once he bit through his ear; but Billy remained confident that all this was a form of play, and not done out of aggression. As he himself wrote, 'It never occurred to me to be afraid of him, as I never sensed the slightest hostility on his part.'

He was therefore all the more shocked when Prince launched a deliberate attack on the eight-year-old son of his filwan, or elephant-keeper. Billy himself was away in Delhi, and Ganga Ram had gone to the market to collect the leopard's meat. The boy should not have been at Tiger Haven at all, after Billy's edict banning the offspring of workers: Billy had told the father as much, but the man had said that if Prince did threaten to cause trouble, he would be able to deal with it. The boy, who was very good-looking, wanted to be with his father, at work, rather than at home with his mother, and he loved being near the elephant.

In the event the leopard walked up to him as he was cleaning his bicycle, and when the lad poked him with a stick, he pounced, grabbing his victim by the head. Pandemonium ensued, and by the time the father thrust a stick between Prince's jaws, forcing him to release his grip, the boy was seriously injured: his scalp was torn, and his head was covered with blood. At the nearest hospital a doctor diagnosed that his skull had been fractured, and then, intimidated by local agitators, sent him off on a debilitating train journey to a larger establishment. There he began to recover, but then Billy was outraged to hear that the nurses were demanding bribes before they would change the wound dressings. In the end maggots infested the wounds, and two weeks after the incident, the boy was brought back to the first hospital, where he died.

With better care, he might well have survived; but his death furnished Billy's enemies with a dangerous supply of ammunition. The leopard was obviously a menace, they clamoured. It must be put down immediately. The filwan was persuaded to resign. There was talk of an attempt to have Billy prosecuted. Luckily the filwan made a statement to the police saying that the boy had courted trouble by provoking the leopard, and the police chief quashed the threat of legal action.

In Billy's view the whole incident, regrettable as it was, became inflated to ridiculous proportions. He pointed out that about 14,000 people were being killed in traffic accidents in India every year, and yet nobody made a fuss. In a recent railway accident in Bihar, when a train had fallen into a river, nearly 2,000 people had drowned, but nobody had been charged with negligence. Yet if a tiger or leopard killed a single human being, there was an immediate outcry.

Steadfast though he was in Prince's defence, Billy did, as a precaution, build a strong cage at the western end of the Tiger Haven buildings, vowing that if ever the leopard had to be incarcerated, he would live there rather than anywhere else. In fact he had no intention of confining him, and built the enclosure mainly so that he could show it to any officials who might visit.

A chance came soon enough, for a meeting of the State Forestry Board was held at Dudhwa, under the chairmanship of the forest secretary, Prakash Krishen, an old friend. Billy knew that he would be surrounded by a swarm of bureaucrats, but nerved himself to invite the whole gang to come and see an animal which was effectively under sentence of death.

When the official vehicles started pouring in along the dirt road, Billy almost had an apopletic fit. He thought the procession would never end – and indeed nearly fifty people turned out, including the forest minister, his deputy, the forest secretary, his deputy, the chief conservator, the chief wildlife warden and sundry other big shots. Most of them were visibly nervous, as they had never been near a wild animal except in a zoo, and although Prince must have sensed their fear, he behaved impeccably, playing with Eelie, walking in and out of the cars and jumping on their bonnets, before lying on the ground and allowing himself to be patted.

In the space of a few minutes he made numerous friends. As the convoy drove off, Billy felt tremendously relieved – and great was his delight when Prakash Krishen, off his own bat, declared the leopard State property. At one stroke the decision placed Prince beyond the reach of scheming officials and straightforward enemies: he became an official animal, and Billy's reintroduction attempt became an official project. At the point where the track to Tiger Haven branched off the metalled road, he put up a sign saying 'Leopard Project', prohibiting women and children from visiting the farm except in closed vehicles. Hard as the rule was to enforce, it at least gave him some legal protection.

~

Prince still had a long way to go before he mastered the art of living wild. Normally he was too frightened to come down off his machan in the dark, but one night he slipped back to Tiger Haven, stole into one of the sheds and seized a buffalo calf by the muzzle. Billy, awoken by the yells of the milkman, dashed across, grabbed the leopard by his scruff and tried to drag him off. Unable to shift him, he tried to block his breathing by plugging his nostrils with his thumb. When this too failed, he shouted for Ganga Ram, who ran in and shoved a pole between Prince's jaws while Billy belaboured him with a sugar cane stalk. The combined assault proved too much for the leopard: he loosened his grip and dashed out of the hut – only to materialize out of the dark a few moments later, rubbing affectionately against Billy's legs. The incident proved, once again, that wild animals, having no sense of right and wrong, do not harbour resentment.

During their joint expeditions in the jungle, Prince often demanded that Billy should go in a certain direction, by leading off, coming back, giving a nip or a playful lunge, and then leading off again. Bit by bit his hunting expertise improved until, at the age of nineteen months, he made his first major kill – an adult chital hind. When Billy and Ganga Ram found him with the body, he was in a state of some agitation, for although he had managed to kill the deer, he had not been able to open it up and feed on it.

As Billy approached, the leopard rushed at him, jumped on him and dashed back to the kill, then repeated the rapid manoeuvres twice more, obviously asking for help. Yet when Ganga Ram disembowelled the deer, he simply sat watching, then went and had a drink.

In the morning, when the humans returned, they found he had eaten some meat from between the thighs – not from a leopard's usual starting place, which is by the pelvis at the loin. There then occurred an amazing incident. Eelie made a sudden rush at the carcass, drove Prince off, and took over the remains. Billy, expecting the leopard to be fiercely possessive, was astonished, both by the dog's boldness, and by Prince's forbearance. No matter that he was three times Eelie's size: he gave way to her.

In March 1973, at twenty months, Prince was almost fully mature. He weighed over 120 lbs and measured six feet and eight inches between the pegs (the old shikaris' term, meaning from nose to tip of tail). Billy's feelings about him had become thoroughly ambivalent. On the one hand, he wanted the leopard to complete his return to the wild, and vindicate all his own claims that rehabilitation was feasible; on the other, he was loath to contemplate the end of an association which he had found deeply fascinating and rewarding. Sentiment demanded that man and leopard should remain close friends and partners; logic insisted that they should part.

Billy knew that, sooner or later, Prince would go – and so he did. By then Ganga Ram had been replaced by Babu Lal, a man of about twenty-eight, who had been working as a night-watchman, protecting crops in the fields, and who soon proved an exceptionally gifted animal keeper. A man of some intelligence, he took steps to educate himself, learnt a bit of English, and revealed a talent for drawing and painting natural subjects like flowers and peacocks. But it was his affinity with animals that made him indispensable to Billy.

Paradoxically, as Prince became more securely established in the jungle, he returned to Tiger Haven with increasing frequency. In Billy's view, the visits meant that he had worked out a territory for himself, and included the farm within it. Nevertheless, the break was coming. On 24 May 1973 he made two appearances, one in the morning, when he sat on a fallen tree and gazed across the river at the house for half an hour, and the other in the evening, when he walked slowly westwards along the north bank. That was the last Billy saw for the time being of the animal which the *Junior Statesman* newspaper had dubbed 'the Incredible Leopard'.

'Brought up by humans,' Billy wrote later, 'he had adapted to the rules of the forest, but while he was learning he had never wavered in his affection for his master or for the little dog who had always played with him. Now, by departing, he showed me that in nature there is one urge which transcends the call of hunger and fear, and that is the call of a creature's own kind. The pull of the wild had proved stronger than the lure of his association with humans, more powerful even than the attractions of easy meals and the reassurance that my presence had always given him.'

~

Not only had Billy's experiment been vindicated. He himself had learned a great deal about leopards, and, along the way, about tigers. He had shown, among other things, that leopards love water, instead of avoiding it at all costs, as other naturalists had claimed. He had learned that the big cats have some sort of extrasensory perception, denied to humans, which enables them to locate each other over long distances. Above all, he had proved to his satisfaction that leopards are not the treacherous characters portrayed by earlier writers. He had always been particularly annoyed by the verdict of an old-time shikari, Colonel A.I.R. Glasfurd, who served for thirteen years in the Indian Army and wrote, 'The tiger is a gentleman, the leopard is a bounder,' and now he was delighted to have demonstrated that the remark was rubbish.

~

In the intervals of supervising Prince's education, he had turned author. Urgently wanting to let the world know what was happening to Indian wildlife, and in particular what was taking place in Dudhwa, he had written a book designed to raise the awareness and sympathy of outsiders. Part of it was autobiographical, briefly describing his own background and how he had come to farm in North Kheri, but the main sections were about the wild animals of the area and their plight.

Writing did not come easily. Scribbling away in longhand, he passed the manuscript chapter by chapter to Mira, who typed it – she being one of the few people who could decipher his dreadful hieroglyphics – but the result was far from publishable. The trouble was that the author's mind tended to run ahead of his pen: in his writing, his thoughts sometimes came out so compressed as to be barely intelligible, and it was weighed down by far too many scientific terms to be enjoyable.

Nevertheless, the typescript clearly contained an interesting story, and in London Amar found a literary agent who passed it to Macmillan, the publishers. Their response was to send an editor, Caroline Hobhouse, out to Tiger Haven, to go through the book with Billy and reshape it, elucidating the denser passages. Unfortunately, author and editor did not hit it off. Billy found Caroline's editing too drastic – 'too tight', as he put it – and when the atmosphere started to become strained, Mabel had to act as a go-between, asking both sides to give ground.

The upshot was that Macmillan sent out a second editor in the form of Johnny Moorehead, son of the distinguished author Alan Moorehead, whose books about Africa and World War II Billy knew and admired. Johnny also stayed at Tiger Haven, loved it, got on capitally with Billy, and soon had the text in shape. The only snag was that the French photographer Michel Arnaud, who came out to take pictures for the book, could not find any tigers, and had to go to Kanha to obtain the necessary shots.

Tiger Haven was published in the autumn of 1973, and Billy made the long haul to London for the launch. Before this, however, another golden opportunity had come his way.

SIX

HARRIET & JULIETTE

Prince had vanished; but Billy felt certain he was still alive, and he was eager to find him a mate. Aiming high, he decided to approach Mrs Gandhi for help. At that stage he was on very good terms with her, and sometimes in Delhi he went to see her at her private house. Once, however, when he began a letter 'Dear Indira,' she did not answer, and thereafter he stuck to more formal modes of address – 'Dear Madam Prime Minister', or 'Dear Shrimatiji'.

He had already sent her an advance copy of *Tiger Haven*, and he had been much encouraged by her reply, dated 16 July 1973:

> I'm delighted to have your beautiful book. I have been deeply concerned about saving our tiger. Any imaginative plan to preserve wildlife has my unreserved support. Our main problem is to create the right public consensus. I hope your book will help in this.
>
> Yours sincerely, Indira Gandhi

Writing again, Billy asked if she could help him obtain a female leopard cub, and by an extraordinary stroke of luck she had just been presented with a pair of orphans from Bihar. Rather than send them to a zoo – which would have been her only alternative – she gave them to Billy. 'You are most welcome to come and collect the female,' wrote Moni Malhoutra, Deputy Secretary in the Prime Minister's Office. In fact both were female, and in Delhi, on his way to London, Billy went to the zoo's veterinary hospital, where he found two scrawny grey kittens, about two feet long, confined in a small cage, 'highly strung, and not much loved by their temporary keepers'.

Every day for a week he visited them, spending time with them in an open-air enclosure, and they gradually started to recognize him. Then one evening at a party in Delhi he met two lively young women, Harriet Gilmour, who was working for the British Council, and Juliette Chubb, daughter of his old friend Henry Thomson, whom he had once courted. When they showed interest in the baby leopards, he said, 'All right, I'll call them after you' – so the cubs became Harriet and Juliette, and Billy left Babu Lal in charge of them while he was away in England.

In London he stayed with Amar, who did all she could to smoothen his path, but, because she was working, had to leave him to his own devices during the day. He hated the metropolis. He had been to London once before, on his way back from a conference in America, but whereas he had managed to navigate his way around the concrete jungle of New York, with its grid pattern and logical numbering of streets, he found the haphazard arrangement of London incredibly confusing, and was constantly getting lost. The roar and stink of traffic, the lack of greenery, the hordes of people – all formed a deplorable contrast to the tranquillity of Tiger Haven.

Nevertheless, his trip reaped a substantial harvest, in that he met the millionaire gambler and zoo proprietor, John

Aspinall – 'Aspers' to his friends. It was Amar who made the initial contact. She had read an article by Aspinall in the *London Evening Standard*, which carried a photograph of him swimming with tigers. Knowing Billy's passionate interest in big cats, she rang up Howletts, one of Aspinall's twin zoos in Kent, got his wife Sally, and explained about the Dudhwa tigers, and her brother's efforts to protect them. Sally told her that Aspers had been born in Delhi, and immediately asked her to come down.

Thus Amar got her first taste of the awe-inspiring luxury in which the Aspinalls lived – lobster, champagne, wonderful silver and glass on the table. She also met John's mother, whose real name was Mary but who, since her second marriage to Sir George Osborne, had been known in the family as 'Lady O'.

Tiger Haven received some excellent reviews. 'One can only hope that this moving and reasonable appeal for the tiger will touch the conscience of his own people,' said *The Daily Telegraph*. In America, where the book was published by Harper & Row, the *Washington Post* reviewer described Billy as 'a civilized person with a fierce, exquisite love of the victimized wild', and went overboard with excitement: 'An extraordinary, utterly fascinating book ... a treat, a revelation, a classic.'

It so happened that in London *Tiger Haven* came out at the same time as Aspinall's autobiographical *The Best of Friends*, and from the same publishers, Macmillan; so it was inevitable that Billy should visit Howletts.

After introductions and a sumptuous lunch, his host went into a cage to fraternize with a big male tiger called Indus, along with one of his keepers, a young man called Nicky Marx. When Billy called, 'John – can I come in?' Aspers sounded rather doubtful, but then said, 'All right. This fellow's reliable enough. Come along.'

A moment later Indus shoved his great head into Billy's crotch, then reared up on his hind legs, to put his paws on Billy's shoulders. Aspers shoved the tiger away, and Billy beat a quick retreat. Afterwards he realized that it was foolish of him to have gone in at all, and he said, 'John, that wasn't fair on either you or me, or on the tiger. If I'd been mauled, the tiger would have got a bad reputation, and you'd have been blamed. So you should never have agreed.'

Edgy as it seemed, that was the start of a friendship which lasted to the end of Aspinall's life. Recognizing Billy's absolute dedication to the animals of Dudhwa, he backed him for ever afterwards with unfailing generosity, regularly sending money to finance conservation projects, and writing in support when heavyweight argument was needed. To Billy, Aspinall was 'not like a normal human being. He was a kind of bridge between animals and men. In many ways he was like an animal – for instance he took it for granted that the male was dominant. You or I would let a lady sit in the front seat of a car, and get in the back, but Aspers always went straight into the front, leaving Sally, or whoever was with him, to sit behind. It wasn't an act – just his natural behaviour. Because he didn't think that animals were in any way inferior to humans, he considered animal behaviour acceptable.'

Billy had found a powerful new friend – and he also acquired a most useful assistant in the form of Nicky Marx, who, like all Aspinall's keepers, had been encouraged to play with tigers in their enclosures, and so already had a good knowledge of big cats. With characteristic generosity, Aspers later sent Nicky out to work, and gain experience, for a year at Tiger Haven.

Back in India, Billy arranged for his new leopard cubs to be put on the train to Lucknow, and met them there. At Tiger

Haven he made them a base in one of the bathrooms, where they slept on a pile of straw, and one of his first priorities was to introduce them to Eelie, who had been living at Jasbirnagar while he was away. Already, at eight months, they were bigger and heavier than the bitch, and he was afraid they might gang up on her, so for a couple of days he kept her in an enclosure, with the leopards free outside.

He need not have worried. As soon as he released her, all three played together equally, and soon Eelie took charge, like an elder sister, egging the cubs on with pieces of rope or burlap for them to chase. Whenever play became too rough, she would snap at them, and they would tumble over each other in their eagerness to get away from her. Often they stalked her, creeping noiselessly up on her from behind; but if she happened to turn and see them coming, they would immediately look away, as if to pretend that an attack was the last thing on their minds. Both sisters seemed to depend less on Billy's company than Prince had, and they were never inhibited by the fear of the jungle which had kept him at home: from the start, they were happy to go exploring, even though they too had an instinctive dread of tigers.

Next to arrive at Tiger Haven were three female wolf cubs, brought from Sitapur by Nicky Marx, at his suggestion. One promptly escaped, never to be seen again, but the two survivors gave their keepers a fine run-around. Even Billy was forced to admit that they proved intractable. Nicky did his best to win their confidence, but in spite of all his attempts at fraternization – sleeping in their cage at night, sitting with them by day – they simply ran away if they saw him coming.

The only person who established real contact was Eelie, who took them bones and regurgitated food for them out of the corner of her mouth. When they escaped from their cage, she began to play boisterous games with them, chasing them about and knocking them over. Later the leopards joined in, and often on his early-morning run along the river bank Billy would be accompanied by all five of the gang – two wolves, two leopards and a dog. His hope was that, with Eelie acting as tutor, the wolves would adapt fully to life at Tiger Haven and settle down there; but when the monsoon broke, one fell ill and died – possibly poisoned, or bitten by a snake – and the other disappeared, never to be seen again.

Serious as he was about the education of his big cats, Billy loved the occasional buffoonery in which his animals indulged. All behaved like idiots from time to time, but for years the chief clown on the premises was Abu Bakr, a cream-coloured goat which he originally bought as a bait for Prince. In the old shikar days goats had been used as the standard bait for leopards, because their bleating attracted the carnivores, and now Billy hoped that Abu Bakr would bring Prince back into range of his camera.

The goat's name, based on the Hindustani word bakri, meaning billy-goat, had derisive connotations, for the original Abu Bakr was one of the founder-imams of Islam, and the animal, with his long white beard, did sometimes put people in mind of an unkempt priest. Yet he managed to escape death at the jaws of a leopard or tiger by refusing to bleat when left alone in the forest. Instead of calling, he would simply curl up and go to sleep – and in the end Billy granted him an indefinite reprieve.

At Tiger Haven he paraded about in front of the buildings, delighting (or appalling) visitors with his party trick of urinating over his back and on to his own head – a habit which formidably increased his already noisome smell. Deeply frustrated by the lack of female company, he would approach humans, or buffaloes, with throaty gargles of passion, and when he received a rebuff, he would respond by putting in a charge. In spite of such reckless advances, he survived for years.

Of all the men Billy employed as trackers, none was more skilled than the one known as Jackson. He came from Panhapur, a district some sixty miles to the south-west, and was from a Christian family.

His real name was Johnson Charan, but his rather squashed face was so strongly reminiscent of Beatrix Potter's Jackson Toad that Jackson he became – although he himself never understood the reason for the change. He arrived at Tiger Haven as a lowly cane-stripper, but when he showed interest in Billy's animals, and a natural ability at handling them, he was taken on as a tracker. At one point the two fell out, and Billy sacked him, but he took him back, and Jackson played no small part in the upbringing of the leopards, and of Tara the tigress. Then, of his own volition, and in spite of Billy's attempts to persuade him to stay on, he left again.

Meanwhile Billy had given his son Suresh some land to cultivate, and after a couple of years Jackson returned for the second time, to act as night watchman over his son's crops. By then, however, he had succumbed to the demon alcohol, and one night, after he had been drinking in the fields, he fell into the fire, was too fuddled to get out of it, and burned himself so badly that he died in hospital. Yet his family connection with Tiger Haven continued, for in due course his grandson Jagdish – always known as 'Haplu' – became Billy's driver.

~

As the leopards grew, major developments were taking place on the conservation front. On the last day of 1973 Moni

Malhoutra wrote to Billy from the Prime Minister's Office with a momentous piece of news:

> The prime minister has written to the chief minister (of U.P.), requesting him to give the whole of the North Kheri forest division the status of a National Park, with the present Dudhwa sanctuary forming its sanctum sanctorum. In recognition of the work you have been doing, she has also asked the chief minister to give you every encouragement. Could you wish for a better New Year's gift?

'No!' was Billy's emphatic answer. This was a tremendous advance, and one for which he had long been campaigning. That same day, 31 December 1973, Mrs Gandhi herself wrote to the chief minister, asking him to, 'give every encouragement to Arjan Singh. He has ploughed a lonely furrow for many years. It is easy to come by armchair conservationists, but rare indeed to find a man with the dedication and perseverance to act in support of a cause which he loves.' Privately, she told Billy that it was entirely because of his work that she had ordered the Dudhwa park's creation.

Fired up by her support, Billy tried to persuade her of the need to restructure the wildlife service. He pointed out that sanctuaries needed specialized management, and that at the moment forest officers were being posted to wildlife jobs without any particular aptitude for the work. He proposed that in the sanctum sanctorum – the core of the new national park – no commercial forestry should be allowed, and that there should be an absolute ban on the auction of minor forest produce such as firewood and coarse grass for thatching. He also called for the establishment of a buffer zone five miles wide all round the park, in which no shooting of any kind would be allowed.

In July 1974, when the authorities were proving slow to implement the order creating the national park, he wrote to Mrs Gandhi again:

> The U.P. Government are very reluctant to take a step which will involve them in financial losses owing to the closure of major and minor forestry operations ... The political pressure brought to bear by border villages is very great, and human intrusion is increasing ... Fires started by these human intruders are highly destructive to the timber value of the forests. It is my firm reading that unless we can have areas where wildlife has precedence over humans, we must lose our wild animals in the near future.

On his own home front, however, the news was more cheerful – and he had conceived a bold new idea:

> The leopards ... are splendid specimens. I would now like to make a similar effort with a young tigress. Apart from the novelty and interest of such an experiment, I do believe that, judging by the trends in the Project Tiger areas, such a process of rehabilitation may become a necessity in the future. I suggest that the tigress should be from three to six months of age, and should be a direct gift from you. Indeed, it could be called Indira, or any other name you suggest.

Once again the prime minister said that she liked his idea, and promised to instigate a hunt for a suitable tiger cub. For the moment none could be found, and in any case Billy had his hands full with the leopards.

The beginning of 1974 was a sad time for the family, because in January Billy's mother, who was eighty-six and already frail, fell seriously ill at Tiger Haven and became bedridden. As the medical facilities at Pallia were so poor, Billy and Balram decided to take her to hospital in Lucknow. Her spirit was still indomitable – for, just before she left Tiger Haven, which she had always loved, she said to Jackson, 'Don't worry. I'll be back tomorrow.'

In Lucknow she went first to the Balrampur Hospital, then to the military hospital, and finally to the home of friends, Begum Ghulam Husain and her daughter Nishoe. Amar flew out from England specially to nurse her, and cared for her devotedly for six weeks, backed up by Billy and Balram. Billy, greatly distressed by her suffering, suggested at one point that it would be kindest to 'put her out', but in the end she died naturally at 5 p.m. on 26 February, the day before Balram's birthday.

Before lapsing into her last long silence, she had asked that her body be cremated at Tiger Haven, and Billy insisted that her wishes should be carried out. Having sent word ahead to warn the staff at the farm, he and Balram therefore set off from Lucknow at 9 p.m. and drove through the night, Billy with the coffin in the Thompsons' big saloon car, Balram following in the jeep.

By the time they reached Tiger Haven at 3 a.m., Billy was so exhausted that he overshot the turning off the main road, but he found that at the farm Nicky Marx had everything organized, and the fire in the drawing-room was blazing to welcome them. The staff had already built an oblong pyre on the beach beside the Soheli, decorating it beautifully with leaves from the forest.

Later that morning a large number of friends gathered from far and wide, among them Jim and Creina Stevens, and the Thompsons. Billy and Balram were both too distressed to conduct a funeral service, but when Amar read out passages from the Prayer Book, Henry Thompson found that she spoke the words so beautifully that they moved him to tears. So passed a formidable matriarch, whose last coherent words had been, 'I've had wonderful children and grandchildren – a wonderful family – but now it's time for me to go.'

~

Only someone who spent a good deal of time at Tiger Haven could appreciate the dedication with which Billy worked. For day after day, week after week, month after month, he and Eelie combed the jungle, searching for evidence that Prince was still alive. Clad in his habitual uniform of short-sleeved shirt, shorts, knee-length stockings and army-type boots, and carrying a hefty stick, he would tramp the forest paths – and not as silently as some of his visitors would have liked.

The young Nepalese conservation scientist K.K. Gurung was faintly irritated at being cautioned to move quietly, and then finding that Billy – as clumsy with his feet as with his hands – crashed along like a small elephant. Not that silent progress is easy in that environment, for, unlike Western species which shed all their leaves during the autumn, the jungle trees, like sal and teak, shed continuously throughout the year, so that, except in wet weather, the ground is always covered with crackly fallout.

Not only did Billy walk hundreds of miles on regular patrols: he tethered goats as bait, sat up over them all night, and hurried to inspect the kills of wild animals which Jackson reported. At last, after numerous near misses and inconclusive glimpses, he got what he had been longing for – an absolutely positive identification, when the leopard returned to a kill at dusk, and Billy, crouching in a hide, met him face to face, unmistakably the animal he knew so well:

> It was a tremendous moment. I did not move or call him, for I knew that our ways had parted, and that it was too late to re-

establish the bond between us ... At the sight of his expression, which I remembered so well, my mind flew back to all our days together. But the light was dying fast, and when a muntjac barked over to my left, Prince withdrew stealthily to the east, disappearing like a beautifully-camouflaged shadow into the deeper shadows of the jungle.

~

The great question, now, was whether he would mate with either or both of the desirable young ladies whom Billy had brought to his patch. By June 1974, at fifteen months, they had grown into beautiful, sleek animals. Juliette was relatively thickset and well-formed, with a deep, old-gold background to her coat. Until then Harriet had been rangy and more lightly built, with a silky, off-white background, but recently she had put on strength, and now weighed 77 lbs to her sister's 72 lbs. She was also the gentler of the two, and to Billy seemed more mature. Anxious as he was to establish them at Leopard Haven, deep in the jungle, he considered that they were still too young, and too much at risk from attacks by tigers, so he continued to give them the freedom of the farm.

Until then his own existence at Tiger Haven had been almost as solitary as a tiger's, for except when his mother came to stay, he had been living on his own, apart from his servants, trackers and farmhands. But in February 1973 things had changed when Balram and Mira abandoned Calcutta to come and live permanently at Jasbirnagar, only half an hour away. After a long stint at the trading firm Balmer Lawrie, Balram had been passed over for promotion and had moved to another company, Shaw Wallace. But then, at the age of forty-seven, he decided he had had enough of commerce and moved out into the country, not least so that he and Mira could give Billy a hand if tourism became established in Dudhwa.

Pallia was then a one-horse place, and shopping facilities were so poor that Balram and Mira would go to Lucknow once a month – a five or six-hour drive each way – to collect stores. Jasbirnagar itself was still primitive, and lacked even a generator: on summer evenings, because it was too hot indoors, the family would sit out on the verandah in the dark. For years Balram missed his city life and friends – so much so that at one point he tried to go back and find another job. Gradually though, he became more interested in the farm, and ran it well.

Meanwhile the leopards' fame had spread over the border into Nepal. There one of the pioneers of wildlife tourism, Jim Edwards, had set up the firm Mountain Travel in Kathmandu and started a successful enterprise in Chitwan – the Tiger Tops hotel, built on stilts on the lines of Tree Tops in Kenya. In the summer of 1975 Survival Anglia Television sent their ace cameraman Dieter Plage out to Nepal to make a film, and Jim suggested they should go down to Dudhwa to meet Billy and see the leopards. He therefore sent a telegram proposing a visit. Later he learnt that his initiative was received with some reserve, as Billy was wary of mass tourism and the disturbance it might cause. What swung things in Jim's favour was the fact that his telegram arrived signed GIN EDWARDS, and Balram, to whom gin was essential daily fuel, decided he must be a good egg.

The visitors much enjoyed a visit to Ghola, where they saw swamp deer, chital and hog deer, and Dieter was touched by the closeness of Billy's relationship with Harriet. 'He is totally dedicated to what he is doing,' he recorded in his diary. Jim was much impressed when Billy took them out into the jungle on Sitara, and they came on two men illegally cutting firewood. Billy at once slid to the ground, went up to the intruders, yelled at them, and, when they shouted back, grabbed them and banged their heads together before hurling them bodily to the ground. As the men scuttled away, Jim asked if such tactics might not provoke retaliation – to which Billy replied, 'Well – if they send more people around, I'll do the same to them.'

In fact, this kind of riposte did nothing for Billy's local reputation – and some people felt that in his dealings with forest officers he blackened his own name by being hasty and arrogant. If, whenever an incident occurred, he had taken more time to explain his point of view, and to conceal his own contempt for the incompetence of officials, his path might have been smoother. His friend and admirer M.K. Ranjitsinh admitted that Billy 'is sometimes his own worst enemy', and that 'he would have helped his own cause by being more diplomatic. But then he would not have been the one-man institution that he is, and the world would have been poorer for it.'

As the young leopards approached sexual maturity, Prince was drawn more and more to the farm, and numerous encounters took place, some of them explosive. By then Harriet and Juliette were generally sleeping in Gran's Cage, but one night Harriet stayed out, and Billy went to bed as usual on the verandah, which was wired-in with fine, mosquito-proof mesh. At one point during the night he half awoke, sensing that something had shaken his bed, but he had a blanket pulled over his head against the cold, and dropped off again without investigating. Only in the morning did he find from the marks in the dust that Prince had come back and sat down against the outside of the mesh.

Another night he was woken at 1 a.m. by a hollow growl. He leapt out of bed and ran to Gran's Cage. Juliette was inside, and when he called Harriet, she appeared from the direction of the Junction Bridge much agitated, giving sharp exhalations and abrupt calls. Since she would not go into the enclosure, Billy spent the rest of the night guarding the end of the bridge, and the leopard went up on to the roof of the house. Daylight revealed that she had suffered several wounds in a clash with a male leopard, probably Prince. Even though such nocturnal disturbances increased, Billy continued to sleep in the open.

All through 1975 the sisters' hunting prowess gradually advanced – and so did their sexual development. Harriet came into season for the first time on 29 January, and Juliette followed almost at once. For four days they indulged in a great deal of rolling on the ground, presenting their backsides and continuously giving hollow growls; but then, to Billy's alarm, they became very restless, and kept wandering off eastwards to the area of the Dudhwa rest house – the one place where he did not want them to appear.

Local opposition, already simmering, increased sharply when Harriet scratched a two-month-old baby, whose parents had brought the child to Tiger Haven in defiance of Billy's ban. In March both leopards again strayed to the east, and one was seen outside the rest house, setting off a spate of gossip. By ill chance the divisional commissioner happened to be in residence, and ordered his guard to shoot the animal, but fortunately the man ignored the instruction.

One after another the scandalmongers claimed to have seen the leopards at times when Billy could prove they had been at Tiger Haven. The forest staff at Sonaripur, eight miles to the east, beyond Dudhwa, alleged that one of his leopards had killed a calf, a goat and four puppies, and had mauled two calves, which had survived. When he went to investigate, he found from the pug marks that the marauder was a sub-adult tiger, which he surmised was struggling to survive on its own, having lost its mother.

He did everything possible to safeguard his two star charges, assuring the forest staff that they were harmless to humans, emphasizing that if anyone saw a leopard, he himself would come at once and take it away, and reiterating that Harriet and Juliette had been specially presented to him by the prime minister. Yet he knew that none of this would be much of a defence 'against minds buttressed by prejudice', and he had an awful premonition that something terrible was about to happen.

He also had a wire-mesh cage built into the back of his jeep, so that if necessary he could shift the leopards in a hurry, and after he himself had seen Harriet sitting on a knoll, contemplating the road-barrier at the entrance to the Dudhwa compound, he decided after all to move both her and Juliette to Leopard Haven. One evening he and Babu Lal took them to their new headquarters and left them sitting on the platform. For the next few days they kept returning to Tiger Haven, and Billy fed them there, but took them back to Leopard Haven for the night. Then, on 18 April, he had to go on a trip to Delhi.

Next morning Babu Lal and Jackson found the machan empty, but tracks showed them that both leopards had walked eastwards, past the farm towards the main road and the railway. They came on Harriet near the railway bridge, but there was no sign of Juliette, and in the morning, when they still could not find her, they set out on another search. At about 10.30 a.m. the cawing of crows attracted them to the bank of the river some 400 yards east of Tiger Haven, and there she was: Balram discovered her lying dead in shallow water by the bank.

When Billy heard what had happened, he was greatly shocked and depressed, for traces of an alkaloid poison were found in samples taken from her body, and he became almost certain that she had been poisoned deliberately, in reprisal for the attack on the calves at Sonaripur, which had taken place only four days earlier. He felt as though he had lost a child, and his grief was compounded three weeks later when the range officer at Sonaripur shot the wretched weakling tiger – the animal whose attacks had touched off the campaign against the leopards.

What distressed him particularly was that the range officer had killed the tiger without proper authority, in defiance of the law. When he pointed out that a million dollars had been subscribed from all over the world to save the tiger, and insisted that action was needed 'to prevent the animal being destroyed by little men in authority who ignored what the law explicitly stated,' an atmosphere of hatred quickly built up.

In a letter to Mrs Gandhi, written in May 1975, a month after Juliette's death, Billy lamented the fact that no action had been taken against the range officer, but that his superior, the divisional forest officer, had made the issue of the ailing tiger a personal one. 'The forest territorial staff, with whom I have lived in peace, are now encouraged in petty forms of harassment,' he wrote. 'A campaign of vilification and calumny has been carried on against me by a local paper.'

His immediate fear was that Harriet also would pick up poisoned bait, and he reckoned that his most urgent duty was 'to defend her from human enemies'. At the same time, he was anxious to continue with her rehabilitation, and to get her mated. He therefore adopted a compromise, sometimes shutting her in at night, and frequently retrieving her by jeep from Bhadraula, at the entrance to the Dudhwa sanctuary.

Fortunately her sexual development proceeded fast, and she began to mate with Prince in a series of nocturnal assignations. At first she did not conceive, and she started making amorous advances to Billy, who found himself obliged to sleep in the wolves' cage – it being too hot indoors – to escape her attentions. One morning innumerable pug marks and rolled-down patches in the dust showed that during the night the leopards had mated right outside the house, only a few yards from where he was asleep, but so silently that he never heard a sound. This taught him that leopards do not advertise their affairs, as tigers do, by roaring and growling. The master-predators, having no natural enemies powerful enough to take them on, can afford to broadcast to all and sundry; but leopards, by doing so, would render themselves vulnerable to attack by tigers, and so keep quiet.

Still wanting to get a photograph of Prince in the wild, Billy decided to spend a night on the Double-storey Machan – and it turned out to be one that he never forgot. Early in the night Harriet, whose voice he recognized, called three times from close at hand. Thereafter silence reigned for half an hour and,

> Then suddenly the whole machan shook as some large animal climbed swiftly on to the lower storey. I sat rock-still. Next I heard a long inhalation, right beneath me ... The machan began to shake again as the animal climbed the ladder to the top storey and stood on the ledge outside the wire-netting walls, peering through. Against the black background of the night-forest I could make out the shape of a leopard, blacker still. At once I knew it was Harriet. She was growling softly, and trying to get inside.
>
>   What she would have done if she had succeeded, I do not know. But I did not fancy the idea of having an amorous leopard inside such a small enclosure. Even if she had remained calm, her attentions would have been unwelcome enough; but if she had panicked, I might have been in severe difficulties. So I took

a lace out of one shoe and tied up the latch of the door, which was loose.

For the rest of the night Harriet stayed on the lower storey, except when she made sallies up the ladder in renewed attempts to join her mentor, and only when dawn was breaking did she go down and walk to Tiger Haven, where she and Billy had a friendly and relaxed reunion.

Her multiple matings with Prince did in the end bear fruit – but her first pregnancy turned out to be a false one, and she aborted not even a half-formed foetus, merely a lump of flesh about two inches long and half an inch thick.

Soon she resumed her encounters with Prince, but before she could conceive, she perpetrated a horrifying incident. It happened during the monsoon, when Billy was away in Delhi on urgent business, and Tiger Haven was cut off by the floods. In defiance of the ban on bringing children to the farm, one of the labourers had imported his small son: not only that, he had failed to keep the door of his room closed, as ordered. Early one morning the leopard found the door open, went into the dark room, discovered the boy lying on the floor, and seized him by the throat. His father rushed to rescue him, but his jugular vein had been punctured, and he died in hospital.

Billy, greeted by this dire news on his return, was both angry and anxious: angry with the father, for having taken such risks, anxious to find out why Harriet had behaved so out of character. He thought that perhaps she had become frustrated at being hemmed in by flood water, and maybe had been overcome by claustrophobia in the confined space of the hut, as Prince had when he attacked Billy in the machan.

When he set off across the river with Babu Lal in an attempt to find her, he was thoroughly nervous, not knowing how she would treat him – but after he had called her a few times in vain, she resolved all his doubts:

> Babu Lal suddenly cried, "Here she comes!" I looked up, to see her running down the slope. She hopped into the boat and absolutely overwhelmed me with affection. First she rubbed herself against me like a huge domestic cat; then she put her paws on my shoulders and started grooming my head. As her rough tongue rasped over my hair, I felt my eyes fill with tears of pleasure and relief. She had not changed in the slightest.
>
> In that wonderful moment I finally realized how absurd it is to attribute human feelings or values to the great cats. Obviously Harriet felt no trace of guilt about what she had done to the child. How could she? To her, killing was a natural, life-giving activity. Her ancestry and instincts had equipped her to do precisely what she had done when she found the boy on the floor. We humans should have prevented the situation arising.

Local people would have endorsed that last remark wholeheartedly. Many pointed out that the boy would not have died if Billy had not given Harriet the free run of the premises, and the accident naturally led to fresh uproar among his critics, who were incensed by his unsympathetic attitude. Yet nothing would deflect him from his purpose: he did not mind if people thought him callous, for his attention, now, was focused on the question of whether or not Harriet would conceive.

SEVEN

THE CUBS ARE BORN

In the spring of 1976 he watched eagerly for signs that Harriet was pregnant, and in April he was at last rewarded. Although her belly looked no bigger than usual, her movements became slower and her nipples were enlarged. Her behaviour also changed: instead of wandering widely in the jungle, she returned to the farm for meals every day, and spent most of her time close by. Anxious as he was that she should have her cubs in the forest, rather than in the house, Billy repeatedly took her across the river to the Escarpment Machan, which he had turned into a form of maternity ward by having a wall of wainscoting nailed round the edges of the platform.

Mike Price, the Survival Anglia cameraman, was at the farm, and eager to film the cubs' arrival, but Billy vetoed the idea, on the grounds that the intrusion might upset Harriet. On the morning of 27 April, when birth was clearly imminent, he was in such a fever of anticipation that, having visited Harriet himself at 10.30 a.m. he sent a messenger over the river at 11.45 to check her again. Back came Babu Lal with the electrifying news that two cubs had been born, and it was all

Billy could do to restrain himself from going across immediately. He managed to wait until 4 p.m., then went over in the boat and climbed the ladder to the machan. Harriet greeted him with a soft growl and a hiss, so he kept his distance, but he was entranced by the two little bundles of spotted grey fur huddled comfortably against their mother.

For four days all went well: tracks showed that the resident tigress had passed beneath the tree platform, but Harriet did not seem alarmed, and she received human visitors with aplomb. Then, as Billy was climbing down from the machan, there was a loud crack, and he saw that one of its supporting legs had almost snapped. In the morning he sent Babu Lal and three other men to repair it, but Harriet appeared in such a bad mood, spitting and snarling and threatening to attack, that the gang withdrew. In the evening, to his dismay, Billy found the machan deserted.

Harriet returned to Tiger Haven for a meal, and a search discovered the cubs in a ravine, some fifty yards from the machan, crawling around in a hollow. The site was so exposed that Billy made several efforts to transfer the family to somewhere safer, but Harriet frustrated all attempts by moving the cubs on herself, until she found a home in another ravine, where she established a secure base in a hole under the roots of an asna tree. Still she came to Tiger Haven for a meal every day, but she spent much of her time with the babies, and Dieter Plage, who had come down again from Chitwan, was able to film the family extensively from the opposite bank of the gully.

Everything changed with the sudden return of Prince, who arrived during the night of 15 May. His presence seemed to unsettle Harriet, who began staying away from her cubs at night, sleeping on the roof of the house and refusing to return

to her den, even when led there by Billy or Babu Lal. After a
while Billy realized that what to him were the menacing hours
of darkness 'must to her be the protective velvet of night, in
which the scentlessness of the cubs, in their secluded den, was
the best possible form of defence.'

Then, on 26 May, everything changed again. As Dieter
filmed and Billy watched, Harriet strode down into the den,
emerged with a cub dangling by its neck from her mouth,
brought it across the river via the flyover of branches, and
deposited it in one of the bedrooms at Tiger Haven. Billy was
astounded, and at a loss as to how to react. Thrilled as he was
to have the cub indoors, at the same time he wanted the family
to have a natural upbringing in the jungle. For the moment
Harriet solved his dilemma by carrying the second cub into a
dense patch of grass across the river, leaving it there, and then
retrieving the first one from the house.

For the next twelve days she kept the family in the grass,
barely a hundred yards from Tiger Haven, coming to the house
for meals, but leaving the cubs out of sight. Trying to fathom
her behaviour, Billy concluded that she was balanced between
two worlds: on the one hand she wanted the cubs to benefit
from the security offered by the buildings, which she knew so
well, but on the other her instincts were telling her that they
should be in the wild.

Soon, however, her best intentions were blown asunder by
the onset of the monsoon. On 7 June the rains broke in fury,
and the river rose so fast that Billy decided, in spite of his
principles, that he must rescue the cubs immediately. Imagine
his agitation when Harriet ate her breakfast meat in the most
leisurely fashion, and loitered about before setting off for the
patch of grass. Back she came, with one sodden cub dangling
from her mouth. Having placed it in her favourite upper room,

she returned to the grass, but to Billy's dismay, she came out again without a burden, returned to the house and proceeded to suckle the first cub, then go to sleep.

Scarcely able to believe what he was seeing, Billy leapt to the dismal conclusion that Cub No. 2 had already been drowned.

Not so. With the water still rising, and the Junction Bridge awash, Harriet at last roused herself, padded off through the downpour, to reappear with the missing infant struggling feebly in her mouth. To cross the bridge she had to wade through ankle-deep water, and all around her heavy raindrops were thrashing the surface into a froth; but she came safe to land, beating the main flood by half an hour.

For the next week the family gave Billy glorious entertainment. When Harriet was with the cubs, they played enchantingly, climbing over her, chewing her ears and tail; but when she went out, they retired into their box and kept so quiet that nobody would have suspected their presence – an instinctive defence mechanism which operated even in the building. Yet after seven days their mother became restive, and started to carry them out, one at a time, in search of other accommodation.

Clearly she wanted to return to the jungle across the river, but the water was still very high, and one morning, carrying a cub, she jumped down into the boat, indicating to Billy in the clearest possible terms that she needed a lift across. He therefore paddled her over, and a nightmare journey it proved, for she kept putting the cub down in the boat's narrow bows, and a dozen times he thought she was going to drop it overboard. Once she had scrambled safely ashore and gone up the escarpment, he waited for her 'faithfully as a well-trained gondolier'; but when she did not reappear, he paddled himself back to the south bank.

Hardly had I reached it when I heard a peremptory aonh! There she was, walking back along the far shore. Aonh! she called, aonh!, aonh!, demanding the return of her private ferry. Back I went. Once more she jumped in. Over we came. Out she hopped. I waited, certain that she would reappear from the house with Cub No. 2.

This time I was right; but before she was ready to leave, she did something very strange. With the cub in her mouth she made a complete tour of the upper storey, jumping from one roof to the next and visiting every corner, as if saying farewell to the place she knew. Then the three of us completed another hair-raising voyage, after which she took her second dangling grey burden off into the jungle.

The most extraordinary feature of the whole episode was Harriet's willingness to use domestic, human rituals to achieve what her instincts told her she must do. Her urge to return her cubs to the wild was compulsive, and came from somewhere deep in her heredity; yet to accomplish the dangerous river crossing, she was prepared to accept my help. This I found extremely moving.

That final tour of the roof-tops made an indelible impression on anyone who saw it, either live or on film. Harriet could – as Billy surmised – have been bidding her old home goodbye; but she could also have been betraying the confusion she felt at being poised between two different worlds. A critic might argue that she had become too imprinted on Billy for her own good.

The next few weeks proved highly fraught, for although Harriet became a model mother, and returned to the secure burrow in the ravine, the Big Tigress began to frequent the area with sinister persistence. Earlier, Billy had heard defensive roars, and deduced that the tigress's own cubs had been killed by a herd of elephants. Did she now, in an instinctive reaction, think that Harriet had stolen her cubs from her? Was she trying to adopt them? Would she kill them if she discovered they were not hers?

One morning, after rain in the night had left the ground soft and made tracking easy, Billy was disturbed to find the deep indentations of the tigress's paws right in the main entrance of the burrow, where she had leant down to peer and sniff inside. He was fairly confident that the marauder had not been able to gain entry, because the gaps between the tree roots were too narrow – but what if she had caught the cubs in the open and eaten them?

Although he found Harriet, she would not – or could not – lead him to the cubs, and he spent a sleepless night, tormented by fears. In the morning, after one fruitless attempt to locate the family, he tried yet again. Leaving Jackson and Eelie behind, he led the way to the burrow, and Harriet followed, constantly hesitating:

> When we reached the den she gazed for a long time at the entrance, and then gave a soft half-call. She repeated the sound once, then again. Suddenly she was answered by what sounded like the chirp of birds. All at once she leapt lightly off the parapet into the entrance: stretching her head and forequarters down into the den, she brought out both cubs. As the two baby faces appeared at ground level, so vulnerable and innocent, a great light shone in my heart and tears trickled down my cheeks. In that moment of joy I realized how little I still understood of the leopards' world.

During those weeks of magic and anxiety, the Survival Anglia team made a wonderful film of mother and cubs. Harriet, of course, was the star – climbing trees, moving around the buildings at Tiger Haven with incomparable grace, bringing up her babies, putting in mock-attacks on Billy and Eelie. Slow motion revealed the amazing agility with which she sprang from one flat roof to another, arching and floating across wide gaps, with her balancing tail stretched out behind, and the extraordinary way in which she pulled her punches. When Billy crouched down and incited her to charge, wearing only a pair of shorts, she would launch herself at him head-on in a flying leap and pivot on his skull, but all the time she kept her claws sheathed, and her huge paws would glide down over his bare shoulders and back like feather dusters, leaving not so much as a scratch. With Eelie it was the same. Harriet would sit up on her haunches and box as the dog charged her, but she made no attempt to knock her little assailant down.

The completed film – *The Leopard That Changed its Spots* – was slightly spoiled (in Billy's view) by the fact that in the middle it switched to Sri Lanka and portrayed leopards living there. The reason was that Dieter felt he needed more variety: the Sri Lankan animals provided him with good material, because they were active during the day, rather than being mainly nocturnal, and the movie included an astonishing sequence in which a family of wild pigs chased and routed a leopard that had attacked them. Billy, of course, would have liked Harriet to have pride of place throughout, and the blood-and-thunder of the Sri Lankan hunt jarred in the middle of the peaceful scenes at Tiger Haven.

Nevertheless, the film was a memorable record of unique events. It has been shown many times on television in England, often at Christmas, and the shots of Harriet carrying her cubs to the safety of the farm have moved countless people to tears.

EIGHT

ENTER TARA

Heavily engaged though he was in trying to protect Harriet and her cubs, Billy was drawn inexorably into the start of his next experiment – the most ambitious and controversial of all – which pitched him into head-on confrontation with the Indian wildlife authorities.

He had long nursed his idea of rearing and releasing a tiger, and in October 1975 he had written again to Mrs Gandhi, reiterating his hopes:

> Dear Madam Prime Minister,
>   My erstwhile male leopard is now completely wild, and I would now like to try a similar experiment with a tiger, as I feel that such a demonstration would prove of value for your Project Tiger. I suggest the initial introduction be made with a tigress, as males are more territorial and intolerant.

A reply from Salman Haidar, Director of the Prime Minister's Office, assured him that 'We are now in pursuit of tiger cubs, and will let you know what happens.' But for six months nothing had happened, and it seemed that no cub could be found in the whole of India. Eventually the breakthrough came via Dieter Plage, who, in the course of a meeting with Mrs Gandhi, was asked if he could help in the search. Soon afterwards, in England, he discovered that a litter of two male cubs and a female was available at Twycross Zoo, in Leicestershire, and he wrote to Billy saying that all three would be his if he would agree to Anglia filming his reintroduction project. With great regret Billy decided that three would be too many – too difficult and too expensive – and asked Twycross to let him know if a single female became available.

Dieter – a German of enormous skill, humility and charm, completely absorbed in his wildlife work – did Billy another priceless service by introducing him to Dr Bernhard Grzimek, president of the zoo at Frankfurt-am-Main, in Germany, and another pioneer conservationist of outstanding achievements. Nearly twenty years earlier, together with his son Michael, Grzimek had made prodigious efforts to record the animals of the Serengeti Reserve in Tanganyika, flying countless sorties over the plains in their zebra-striped light aircraft. In 1959, when Michael was killed in a crash caused by a collision with a griffon vulture, his father commemorated him with his book *Serengeti Shall Not Die*, a moving record of their work together. After Michael's death, Grzimek had more or less adopted Dieter as his surrogate son.

Now he offered to pay for a tiger cub and its transport to India, and his international reputation gave Billy powerful moral support. So it was that in July 1976, when Billy received a message saying that a single female cub was available at Twycross, and asking him to come and collect her, he could not pass up the opportunity. With Harriet and her family menaced by the Big Tigress, there was nothing he wanted less than to leave home at that moment; but the chance might never recur, and so, full of foreboding, he left Babu Lal with a supply of firecrackers and blank cartridges, instructing him to let off a fusillade every evening in the hope of keeping the tigress away, and set off for Europe.

His first port of call was Frankfurt, where he met Grzimek. In London he once again stayed with Amar, and when he proceeded to Twycross, the proprietor of the zoo introduced him to John Voce, the young keeper who had hand-reared the cub. Jane, as they had called her, was then three months old, and to Billy it seemed that her face had a most attractive expression; but when he tried to make friends with her, she was initially hostile, biting and scratching at him until his trousers were torn to shreds and soaked in blood. He concluded that, being used to English people, she did not like his Indian smell, and so he dumped his ruined trousers in her cage, in the hope that she would adjust to them. He had already decided to rename her Tara (Star), after her maternal grandmother, who had been bred by John Aspinall.

For the next two days he sat outside her enclosure in a small, wired-in passage, where visitors gawped at him as if he were some outlandish exhibit. Each evening he returned to London in a car which Survival Anglia had provided for him, and on the third day his patience paid off: the cub rubbed herself against him through the wire netting, and gave him a Prusten – the fluttering of the lips that indicates friendliness. This made him confident that the two of them would get on, and he returned temporarily to London, to finalize arrangements with Survival Anglia.

At Brooke House, the company's offices in Park Lane, he got an unpleasant shock. Five thousand miles away in Delhi the babus were already trying to block him: a telephone call came from Nalini Jayal, Joint Director of the Forest and Wildlife Department, who told Billy that he was on no account to import the cub, as they had heard she was not a purebred Bengal tigress, but had Siberian genes in her ancestry.

Billy's answer was short and fairly sharp. 'This is absurd,' he said. 'All the bookings have been made. And besides, the project has the blessing of the prime minister.' What he did not know was that the alarm had been raised by Paul Leyhausen, Chairman of the IUCN's Cat Specialist Group, who had seen fit to announce at that moment that none of the tigers in European zoos were of pure Bengal strain. Disregarding Jayal's call, Billy carried on with his schedule, and took time off to seek a publisher for a book he had written about Prince. For months he had struggled to write the leopard's story, but after his earlier experiences with Macmillan, he did not feel like returning to the firm. He had become fascinated by Joy Adamson's accounts of her lioness Elsa, especially *Born Free*, which had come out in 1960, and he decided to approach Billy Collins, head of the publishing firm which had brought out the lion books.

He was much impressed by Collins' office, and particularly by the panelled hall of the eighteenth-century house in St James's Place, Mayfair. He never forgot how, as he sat waiting for his appointment, 'the stairs creaked, and down came this tall, good-looking man, full of old-world politeness'. Collins warmed to the idea of the leopards, and passed Billy's typescript to Marjorie Villiers, one of the founders of the Harvill Press, which Collins had taken over.

Marjorie was a brilliant and sympathetic editor – it was she who had created the immensely successful *Born Free*, from the scraps of illiterate text on thin, discoloured paper that Joy Adamson brought her. But when Billy saw some of the work she had done on his own book, he sent Collins what he afterwards admitted was an ill-judged letter, complaining about her rewriting. Back came a fairly curt note, saying that Marjorie was one of the firm's leading editors, and that Billy should perhaps look for another publisher. This early clash was unfortunate, for if Billy had been able to swallow his objections, his books would surely have done well under the Collins imprint.

While he was still in London, dire news arrived from home. One of Harriet's cubs had been killed by the Big Tigress, and the other had drowned when she tried to bring it across the river. As he wrote later, he felt 'sick at heart to think that two such spirited little creatures had had their lives prematurely snuffed out.' He tried to console himself by reflecting that a leopard has no notion of death, and that the animals of the jungle do not fear extinction as humans do. Nevertheless, it was a heavy blow, made all the worse by the fact that for the time being he did not know the details of what had happened.

All he could do was look forward, and late in August he returned to Twycross to collect Tara. Colin Willock, Executive Director of Survival Anglia, had offered the travellers overnight quarters at his own home, which was conveniently near Heathrow Airport, so they spent their first night together there. Tara slept in an empty stable, much to the disgust of the resident Jack Russell terrier, Dudley, who, as interpreted by his master, remarked, 'I've seen some cats in my time, but this is ridiculous,' and refused to go near the stable for a week afterwards.

At 2.30 in the morning the travellers were on the road again, this time to Heathrow, where the cub was loaded into the baggage-hold of a Pan Am jumbo jet, with her cage secured to one of the struts. Billy was loath to leave her there, among all the luggage, but at Frankfurt – the first stop – she seemed perfectly calm, especially after two air hostesses had accompanied him into the hold and given her some milk, which she drank. Milk for the tigress, champagne for Billy in the first-class lounge – and then they were airborne again with a new crew, even more accommodating than the first. Another stop, at Teheran, caused no problems, and soon they were descending into Delhi.

Even Billy, accustomed though he was to babudom, had not been prepared for the bureaucratic obstruction in which he then became enmeshed. Fortunately he had arranged for Babu Lal to come to Delhi, and he looked after Tara in spacious quarters at the zoo, while Billy himself battled his way through thickets of red tape.

From his tracker he at last learnt more about the fate of the leopard cubs. On the morning of 24 July, when Babu Lal and Jackson crossed the river, they had found Harriet, with one cub, up a tree, growling, and as they approached they heard a heavy animal crash away through the bushes. From the evidence – claw marks in the bark of the tree trunk, a broken-off branch, tufts of fur and drops of blood – they were certain that the marauding tigress had caught the other cub and eaten it. Next day Harriet had come to Tiger Haven with the second cub dangling dead in her mouth, and it seemed that she had inadvertently held it under water while swimming the river.

At last, on 17 September, Billy managed to outwit the bureaucrats – and also to avoid paying an importation fee of Rs 16,500 which one of them demanded – and set off for home in a hired station wagon at 4 a.m. The drive to Jasbirnagar took eight hours, and during it Tara acquired some abrasions on her nose and the sides of her eyes, where she had rubbed against the wire mesh of her cage; but otherwise she survived it none the worse, and she completed the final stage of the journey in style, riding through the floods to Tiger Haven loaded, cage and all, on to the back of Sitara, who met them at the river crossing.

Billy's immediate need was to introduce the newcomer to the residents. He was confident that Eelie would accept the cub without fuss, but what of Harriet? Since a tigress had recently killed her cubs, might she not turn furiously on a junior member of the same species? Another danger was that Tara would be attacked by a wild tiger, and before he left he had taken the precaution of getting several of the verandahs wired in, to form cages, so that he now had a relatively secure base.

Eelie acted entirely in character. For two days she and Tara were fed together, with the cub on a lead. On the third day they went walking, still collared. On the fifth day they went loose, and when the tigress leapt on the dog out of sheer exuberance, Eelie bared her fangs, gave her a nip, and so established the order of precedence, which continued in force even when Tara outweighed her by a factor of eight to one.

Reconciliation with Harriet proved more difficult. The leopard was living close to Tiger Haven, across the river, and immediately sensed that an alien creature had arrived. It took her several days to overcome her inhibitions, but her confidence gradually returned, and she came to feed outside Tara's enclosure. As Billy recorded, their first meeting in the open, on the tenth day, was fairly explosive:

As soon as Harriet realized that there were no bars between them, she raced up a teak tree, then immediately came down, ran at Tara and gave her an open-mouthed roar. Tara rolled over and grinned submissively, but roared defensively when Harriet crowded her. Harriet seemed to be aware that this was a cub, and tried to play with her, but now it was Tara who was nervous. When Harriet crept up and ran at her, Tara inclined her head in an ingratiating snarl, before rolling over with a defensive roar as Harriet leapt lightly over her.

Such a melée might have disconcerted handlers less experienced than Billy, but he judged it a promising start – and soon he began taking all three animals for early-morning walks in the jungle. He would lead, usually followed by Eelie, Tara and Harriet, in that order, until the tigress decided to ambush one of the others and reorganize the column. A couple of hours later, back home, the animals would spar among themselves while Billy took a breather. His aim in walking them every day was partly to give them exercise, but also to get Tara used to the forest, and to familiarize her with the immediate range around Tiger Haven. As he wrote later, 'I felt like a modern St Francis of Assisi as I led the way down the jungle pathways.' At the farm Tara would practise her instinctive stalking techniques on one or other of the water buffaloes, creeping up on it behind every available tussock of grass with exaggerated caution, but then, if the bovine great animal turned to look at her, she would spin around and bolt.

When the monsoon floods subsided, Billy extended the daily walks into the jungle north of the river, and within a few weeks he estimated that he had established a range of between thirty and forty square kilometres. As Tara grew, relationships between the species kept changing. For a while Harriet seemed to think that the tigress was one of her own cubs, although rather large, and treated her as such; but when Prince came back into the area and started attracting her again, she became more detached.

Billy quickly saw that his tigress was going to be an expensive guest, and soon after his return he wrote to Grzimek saying that although he had financed the leopard project himself, with some help from the World Wildlife Fund and the Fauna Preservation Society of London, the tiger rehabilitation project was going to cost much more. As if to justify the expense, he reiterated his reasons for going ahead:

> The aim of the project is to demonstrate that tigers born in captivity can be returned to the wild state ... Relocation of living tigers would not increase the population, but would merely entail the movement of an animal from one place to another. It is hoped and expected that the information gained from the project will enable us to increase wild tiger populations, should this prove necessary.

~

Billy worked out that the expenses – for food, vitamins, medicines and a keeper's wages – would amount to some $1,800 a year. He would also need a deep-freeze costing $850 and a safety cage costing $350. Drafts of money would have to be approved by the Reserve Bank of India and remitted to India under the heading of 'scientific Project'.

Writing in reply, Grzimek promised that his society would provide a total of $8,800, over four years – a generous subvention that made the entire scheme possible. Billy's response was to send him regular progress reports, and to invite him to Tiger Haven – but by the time Grzimek eventually came out to Nepal, and Billy met him at Tiger Tops, in Chitwan, he had decided that India's wildlife policies were impossibly regressive, and he simply said, 'I'm not coming.'

At the beginning of December 1976 Billy had to leave home again. Almost always, when he went away, some disaster seemed to strike, and it was with great reluctance that he set out once more on his travels. He had little option, for he had been awarded the World Wildlife Fund's Gold Medal, and the presentation was to be made on 2 December at the closing dinner of the organization's fourth international conference, held in San Francisco.

Leaving Babu Lal in charge, he flew out and back as quickly as he could, not stopping in London on the way. The meeting in California was chaired by Peter Scott, and the citation commended Billy – the only Indian to win the medal – for his 'private initiative and pioneering work for the preservation of the rich wildlife heritage of India, culminating in the establishment of the Dudhwa Wildlife Sanctuary and its proclamation as a National Park.' Outsiders often assumed that it was the creation of the park that brought him the award, but he himself always believed that it was his efforts to save the swamp deer which won him international recognition.

The award brought no money – only the medal and a gold Rolex watch. Back at home, he found that for once nothing untoward had occurred in his absence. Tara grew so fast that by the middle of December she was larger and heavier than Harriet. She also became increasingly rough in her play, and only a man with Billy's powerful physique could have stood up to her boisterous charges. When they went along the path by the river, she often wrestled him down the bank into the shallows, and as he remarked mildly, he wondered how 'weaker people would put up with these playful ways'. Violent as she was, he remained unshaken in his confidence that she would never attack him seriously, and that all her assaults were made out of high spirits. For this reason he was never afraid of her – and she, never sensing fear on his part, repaid him with affection and loyalty.

No matter how obstreperous she became, he went out of his way not to discipline her. Her upbringing, he felt certain, should be the very opposite of that given to circus animals, which were usually cowed into obedience by fear: he was determined not to do anything that might take the edge off Tara's instincts or make her hesitate when, in the wild, she got a chance of a kill. He knew that her very survival would depend on trigger-sharp reflexes that had not been inhibited by earlier punishments. In any case, she always made up for any excesses she had committed by rubbing her great head against his waist, and he felt 'there was no reward as valuable as having gained the affection and trust of such a magnificent creature of the wild'.

His reports to Grzimek reflected his own anxieties. 'There is continual danger that she may be attacked by wild tigers. My main objective is to give her progressive isolation from humans ... The translocation to a more secluded area will be a crucial phase.' Soon he was writing, 'Tara's weight is estimated at between 200 and 250 lbs, tail length 2' 4", body length 5' 2", giving a total length of 7' 6". She is now fed 6 kg of meat a day.'

During the winter of 1976-77 Tara and Harriet still spent a good deal of time together, but the leopard was increasingly preoccupied with Prince, who frequently returned to the area of Tiger Haven, and at one point she went off with him for three days on end. The tigress, meanwhile, continued to develop: she grew new canine teeth, which developed before the old ones fell out, and showed more interest in the animals like pigs or hog deer that she saw in the course of her walks – but since she simply ran after them, as a dog would, rather than stalk them, she could not catch them.

In February Billy received a letter from Laurens van der Post, the writer, traveller and anthropologist, inviting him to a Wilderness Conference to be held in South Africa. Van der Post was hoping to make a film about Tiger Haven, and wrote to ask if Billy would come to the meeting as an honoured guest, and be one of our main speakers. I know what the Indian government feels about South Africa, but there are over a million Indians, among whom I have many friends, in South Africa, and I know they all support this invitation.'

Billy replied that he would love to accept, but that he would need to get a visa – and this, predictably, was not forthcoming, given that India did not recognize the state of South Africa because of its policy of racial apartheid. In June Van der Post wrote again, in disappointment, saying, 'It's a mad, mad world when people of goodwill and like-minded spirit cannot freely foregather whenever they choose, to advance a cause of fundamental concern to mankind.'

For the first few months of Tara's life at Tiger Haven, Billy's relationship with the forest department was fairly amicable, and the young tigress was looked upon as the showpiece of Dudhwa National Park. Press reporters and photographers published a great deal of sentimental rubbish about her, and the park director, R.L. Singh, who fancied himself as a popular author, produced several articles about the project in Hindi newspapers.

But in March 1977 a highly unwelcome change took place in Delhi when, in the general election, Indira Gandhi and her Congress Party were defeated by a coalition of opposition groups which united to form the Janata Party. It was Mrs Gandhi's programme of family planning that caused her downfall: ninety per cent of the voters turned against her. Incredible as it seemed, in Billy's words, 'a vastly over-populated nation had opted for bigger families'. The change of government filled him with apprehension. Not only had he lost his most powerful supporter: he also knew that, in the long term, the greatest danger to tigers would be the ever-accelerating increase in the tide of humanity that was ceaselessly lapping the edges of wildlife reserves.

At home, as the hot weather set in again, a more immediate threat materialized in the form of the Big Tigress, who reappeared close to Tiger Haven with a cub in tow, and one afternoon chased Tara out of the river, where she had been cooling off. From her aggressive behaviour, Billy could tell that the senior animal was trying to push Tara off her own range, and he was all the more anxious for the year-old tigress's safety.

When the monsoon set in, and the land around the house was flooded, the only satisfactory area in which to walk was on the escarpment, across the swollen river, and to reach it he had to ferry his menagerie across – no easy task:

> The only means of making the crossing was by boat, and Tara had her own ideas about how this should be accomplished. After trying to wrestle Babu Lal or myself into the water, she would pretend that she was not interested in the expedition; but once we had boarded the boat, she would land with a flying leap in the centre, nearly capsizing the craft.
>
> Eelie was then coaxed on board, and very wisely sat stolidly in the centre until we reached the other side. Tara restlessly paced the boat, and in her impatience she would lean her ninety-one kilos on the leading oarsman ... Once we had reached the far bank, she would leap off the boat and rush up the escarpment slope, and it was only after she had disembarked that Eelie would step gingerly ashore.

Billy's existence became even more complicated when Harriet again gave birth, this time to a single cub, which she produced on 1 July in a maternity ward that he had specially constructed in one of his upstairs bathrooms. Because the cub was born on a wild and windy night, he called her Mameena, after Rider Haggard's character in *Child of Storm*, and she spent the first three months of her life in the house, while her mother wandered about outside or went off on her own into the jungle. Although she suckled the cub satisfactorily, Harriet surprised Billy by seeming to take very little interest in her. This apparent indifference proved misleading, for when Jackson trapped Mameena in a small cage so that he could take her out to a machan in the forest, he provoked a violent incident:

> Mameena gave a cry of distress, which brought Harriet flying down from the roof. With a roar of fury she charged the partition door. At the second attempt she demolished it and hurtled into the room. Jackson scuttled out and yelled at me to come back to the house as fast as I could. I ran back and found Harriet still highly agitated, snarling and spitting. She even made a half-charge at Jackson.

After that outburst Harriet calmed down, and settled with her cub in the open; but maternity changed her relationship with Tara yet again. Her attitude to the tigress had grown more aggressive, and the fact that Tara became subservient suggested to Billy that the tigress appreciated the situation. Then, after a period of stand-off, during which both avoided each other, Tara started to greet Harriet with a Prusten, and a reunion took place.

With the monsoon at its height, the difficulties of providing the carnivores with enough food became challenging. By far the cheapest way of feeding them would have been to slaughter the occasional buffalo on the premises: a buffalo then cost between 200 and 300 rupees, and each beast would have yielded about 450 lbs of meat. But when Billy applied to the deputy commissioner of Kheri for permission to slaughter, he was refused, so that meat had to be fetched from Shahjahanpur, a round trip of 120 miles. Not only that: with Tiger Haven marooned by floods, the first and last stages had to be made by boat, tractor or elephant. This meant that the journey took at least three hours each way, and by the time the meat reached its destination, most of the ice packed round it had melted. If the public electricity supply had failed – as it often did – the farmhands would have to start up Billy's ancient, crude-oil generator to power the deep-freeze

Yet again one of Billy's brief absences from home seemed to precipitate a crisis. Late in August he had to go to a wildlife meeting in Lucknow, and on his way back he stopped for the night at Sitapur. There, at 5 a.m., he woke from a vivid dream in which he could hear Tara giving distress roars, which were growing fainter, and although he was running towards the sound, he could not close the gap between them.

He thought no more about it until he climbed on to Sitara for the final lap of his return journey, with a cargo of meat for the animals, when he saw Babu Lal approaching with a downcast expression on his face. His news was that Tara had been badly mauled in a fight with a wild tigress. Billy promptly changed his plans. Having sent the elephant on ahead, he drove back to Pallia and called on the local vet. Making excuses, the man took off elsewhere in a hurry, but deputed his trainee to administer tranquillizing and anti-tetanus injections.

The young man was understandably nervous, and his confidence was not increased by having to finish the journey to Tiger Haven on foot, splashing along the bank of the flooded river in pitch darkness, through water sometimes up to his waist, constantly at risk of stepping off the bank into the channel itself. They found Tara licking her wounds, the worst of which were two deep gashes in her right hind leg. Somehow the vet, who showed no mean tenacity, managed to administer three injections, and after a good night's sleep Tara began to recover. But it was more than three weeks before she was fit enough to resume her normal perambulations, and without that prompt medical attention, she might not have pulled through. From Babu Lal and Jackson, Billy learnt that she had been attacked while lying asleep under a bush near the Escarpment Machan, and that her assailant had eventually been scared off by the man stationed on the platform as a security guard beating a tin can.

As Tara grew more mature, it seemed to Billy that she had an elementary sense of humour. Whenever she managed to knock him down the bank into the river, she was clearly delighted, and rushed off with her tail in the air. Yet her hunting skills developed with what seemed to him agonizing slowness, and one night, when she found herself in the middle of a big herd of chital, which had come out to graze on the open fields, she merely raced round and round, unable to catch anything, with the deer apparently sensing her amateurishness and making no effort to escape.

Not until November, when she was nineteen months old, did she make her first kill – and that indecisively. One afternoon Billy heard a deer giving loud distress calls, and, thinking that somehow the Big Tigress might be involved, ran towards the sounds, which were emanating from beyond a patch of tall grass. On the way he was overtaken by Eelie, who disappeared into the grass, and when he came into the open he saw Tara trying to pull a sambar fawn out of the river, where it had taken refuge. A minute or two later, when he crossed the bridge to get a better view, he was amazed to see that Eelie had driven the tigress off her victim, and was standing in the water, nipping at the fawn, while Tara ran up and down the bank in agitation. As soon as he had got hold of the dog and tied her up, Tara regained control and pulled her first kill on to dry land.

For that day and the next, she fed on it; but by the second evening some mysterious form of communication seemed to have spread news of the kill far out through the jungle, because a tiger called persistently to the south. Later that night another tiger blasted off a full-throated roar right opposite the place where Billy was asleep, nearly blowing him out of bed, and in the morning pug marks showed that the mature male tiger known to Billy as Long Toes had walked past.

The proximity of males seemed to accelerate Tara's development. Billy still tried to shut her into her cage every night, to protect her from the Big Tigress, but sometimes she eluded capture and spent the night out. By December, even if she had slept at home, when released in the morning she started calling loudly and went off on her own, instead of keeping Billy company on his walk.

One day in the new year of 1978 she moved off into the grassland to the west, and when Billy heard swamp deer raising the alarm there in the evening, he went in search. For a while his calls produced no response: then Tara appeared from across the river, came up to him, rubbed her head against his waist and gave a soft moan. At that moment another tiger roared, from only 200 yards away, clearly displeased at being left on his own, and Billy felt a shiver of excitement at the thought that Tara had been in contact with him a minute or two earlier. 'Old loyalties and her feed habits had triumphed for the time being,' he wrote later, 'but the bonds were weakening as the summons of her own kind gradually and inexorably took over.'

From that moment she became less and less susceptible to control: every day some instinctive compulsion drew her into the jungle, and Billy felt sure she was spending the time with the young tiger which he had come to call Tara's Male. After one more night in her cage at Tiger Haven, into which Billy managed to lure her with a pig bone, she took off into the jungle, never to return. At the age of twenty months and ten days, she had done what he had always hoped she would do, and answered the call of the wild.

~

Throughout these weeks of ever-increasing tension, Billy had the further problem of trying to keep track of Harriet and Mameena. Try as he might, he could not fathom the mother's behaviour, for she kept leaving her cub alone for days on end, and when the winter weather turned exceptionally cold, he feared it would die of malnutrition or hypothermia. Some mornings Harriet would lead Jackson to the place she had deposited Mameena, but on other days she seemed to take him deliberately in the wrong direction, so that he could give her the food he had brought out.

On Christmas night Billy was awoken by a visitation many other people might not have cared for. As he slept on the verandah, Harriet pushed her face into his, demanding food, which he gave her, and for the next three days, which were atrociously cold and wet, she hung about the farm, sheltering from the rain and coming to be fed three times a day. But where was Mameena? Could the five-month-old cub survive the wintry weather? Billy became convinced that she was dead.

On 30 December, when the weather had cleared, he drove Harriet out to what he thought must be the centre of her range and left her there. It was not until New Year's Day that Mameena eventually appeared, with her mother – the best New Year's gift that Billy could have wished for. Where the cub had been all the time, how the mother communicated with her and kept her under control, he could not determine. His impression was that sometimes Harriet did not know exactly where she had left Mameena, but that once she had reached the general area, she summoned the cub with some signal imperceptible to humans.

She gave another extraordinary demonstration of this ability in the new year of 1978, when Mameena again disappeared for so long that Billy despaired for her life. On 5 February, when Jackson was searching in vain for the cub, Harriet set off north-eastwards, leading him for at least two miles past the Dudhwa forest lodge, over the main road, through the jungle, across the railway line and on past a large pond, until suddenly she stopped, sniffed the air and gave a couple of low grunts – whereupon Mameena sprang out of the undergrowth and bounded to greet her by jumping on her and rubbing noses.

Wondering about the instinct that had guided Harriet back to her daughter, after a separation of at least sixteen days, Billy reflected yet again on how foolish it is to attribute human values to wild animals:

> Perhaps their life, simple as it seems, is yet more complete than ours; their moments of happiness may be brief; but at least they do not experience lingering sorrow. They merely exist, with the inevitability which is at the heart of nature.

~

His chances of learning more of the leopards' secrets were cut brutally short. On 22 May, for reasons he could never discern, Harriet finally abandoned Mameena, and a month later the cub was run over by a train on the Nakauhwa Bridge, where she had been marooned by the monsoon floods. Harriet did not outlive her by long. Having spent much of the summer around Tiger

Haven, she disappeared on 1 November, and ten days later her body was found lying in the grass scarcely a hundred yards from the house, on the far side of the river. She had been dead for several days, and Billy never knew what killed her: it might have been poison, or a snakebite, but, as he wrote, the finality of her death was so awful that he hardly wanted to find out:

> The most pathetic feature was that she had been trying to reach home: mortally stricken, she had struggled almost to her haven, only to die within a few seconds of help. Her death was a shattering blow to me. Tradition says it is unmanly to shed tears, but I am not ashamed to have wept for this most beautiful of cats, who had bestowed such affection on me. For many weeks I could not speak about her without being overcome by emotion. So long had I known her, so much time had I spent with her, so closely had our lives been interwoven, that I felt I had lost a daughter.
>
> We buried her body beneath a shroud on the near bank of the Soheli, close to that of Juliette and only a few yards from Gran's Cage, at the very heart of the territory she knew so well.

NINE

TOURISTS

In December 1973 the U.P. government had created Billy an Honorary Wildlife Warden, which meant that he could, in theory, legitimately take visitors for drives into the sanctuary. For the time being he did nothing in that line, but in 1976 the first tourists arrived at Tiger Haven – a party from the American embassy in Delhi – and from then on, with the help of Balram and Mira, he continued to bring in tourists on a modest scale, as a means of raising money to support wildlife projects. Yet he remained ambivalent about the whole enterprise, fearing that hordes of visitors would create intolerable disturbance within the park.

In any case, it was clear that tourists would never make him a fortune, for relatively few foreign visitors ventured into that area of U.P., and Dudhwa lacked the appeal of more glamorous tiger reserves like Ranthambore and Kanha. The accommodation in its forest rest house was of a standard well below what most tourists would hope for, and there was no decent hotel within reach. Jim Edwards saw that Tiger Haven, with its idyllic situation, could have been extensively developed, with bigger buildings, solar heating, a swimming-pool and so on; but Billy wanted none of this, for he knew that such embellishments would destroy the charm of the place, which, after all, was his home.

Another factor limiting tourism was the weather. During the monsoon, from late June until the end of October, Tiger Haven is definitely unfit for foreign visitors, being often cut off by flood water, and always intolerably damp. In November, as the ground dries out and temperatures fall, conditions become very pleasant. During the cold nights of December and January, with the thermometer sometimes down to 45° F, so much moisture condenses in the air that in the morning the jungle is often enveloped in thick mist, and water drips from the trees, as if rain is falling. February and March are the best months, with nights still cool but the sun agreeably warm during the day. Then in April and May temperatures rise to an increasingly uncomfortable level.

A further inhibiting factor was – and remains – the difficulty of reaching Tiger Haven. It is true that the sheer remoteness of the place is part of its charm, but the 300-mile journey from Delhi is a nightmare – and in the early days it was even worse, as Billy had no telephone or radio over which last-minute changes of plan could be passed.

The most straightforward way to reach Tiger Haven was, and is, to go by taxi, but the roads are diabolical, with only a narrow strip of pitted tarmac down the middle, off which ordinary cars were constantly forced by demon-driven lorries and buses. In the towns, ambling bullock carts, tidal waves of bicycles and rickshaws, sacred cows and surging hordes of pedestrians obstruct progress still further, so that passengers arrive coated from head to foot with dust, and shaken to pieces.

Another alternative is to fly from Delhi to Lucknow, and drive from there – but that still means five hours on the road. A third possibility is to take the night train for Lucknow and disembark at 4.30 a.m. at Shahjahanpur – a hellhole at the best of times – where Billy has a jeep waiting. Even then the traveller is faced with a drive of nearly three hours, much of it in the dark, and some of it through forest haunted by dacoits. The loaded pistol which the driver keeps in the dashboard pocket is not for show.

In spite of these difficulties, people did come, and it was Balram and Mira who masterminded the tourist operation – she with her admirably efficient organization of the house, the meals and the servants, he with his conviviality, his gifts as a genial host and his ability to engage anybody in friendly conversation. Balram never really shared Billy's passionate interest in the animals, but he made himself extremely knowledgeable about them, and became able to answer visitors' questions with authority. He and Mira acquired extensive knowledge of the local birds, which are, by any standard, phenomenal in their variety: more than 400 species have been identified in the Dudhwa area, from the spectacular giant hornbills and crested serpent eagles down to pied kingfishers and tiny bee-eaters.

While Balram and Mira bore the brunt of entertaining visitors, taking them for drives and seeing to their material comfort, Billy was able to carry on with his own ploys, avoiding strange guests as much as he decently could, but playing his role as the wildlife guru whenever he had to. He was well aware of his own tendency to withdraw into himself, and had to struggle to be more sociable.

Drives along the earth roads of the park often brought good sightings, especially at first and last light, when herds of chital would be grazing in open spaces, and a tiger might cross the track at any moment. Everyone lucky enough to get one glimpse of a tiger agreed that it was worth more than a whole morning watching lions in the wide open spaces of East Africa – the environment being much closer, the tiger much more secretive, and harder to spot. During the day, wonderful numbers of birds were active.

Yet the most thrilling part of any visit – for a few favoured visitors only – was a session on the Double-storey Machan, which Billy had built on the south bank of the Soheli within walking distance of the house. On the opposite bank, only twenty yards or so from the platform, was a baiting site on which he tethered buffaloes in the hope that the big cats would come and make a kill, and in a jamun tree above the open space he fixed up a red floodlight which he could turn on or off gradually, by remote control, from across the water.

His objective in baiting was twofold: first, to encourage the major predators to stay in an area that was relatively safe for them, and bring them to a point at which he could monitor them; and second, to give special visitors a better chance of seeing a tiger or leopard, which are notoriously difficult to find in dense jungle. Baiting for tourist purposes was officially discouraged in tiger reserves in November 1973, but in 1979 a new dispensation decreed that it could be used for 'for scientific or special purposes', such as locating and dealing with a maneater. Billy carried on regardless.

Whenever anyone accused him of being cruel to buffaloes, he would retort by asking if the person complaining had ever seen a Muslim butcher at work in a filthy slaughterhouse or yard: to halal a buffalo, the man would have the wretched animal thrown over and held down while he three times invoked the blessing of Allah and tried to cut its throat with a rusty knife while it was still fully conscious, shaking and rolling its eyes with fear. Billy pointed out that buffaloes tethered in the jungle showed no sign of the stress that assails them in a slaughter yard, but lay peacefully chewing the cud; and he was adamant that death at the jaws of a tiger, which kills with a single bite to the throat or neck, was far quicker.

In any event, it was a memorable experience to walk out quietly along the path beside the river and sit on the top storey of the machan, looking out over the water as evening came on. If a tiger had killed a buffalo the night before, the half-eaten carcass would be visible on the ground beneath the baiting tree, with ribs sticking up like the wreck of a stranded ship; but soon darkness seemed to well up out of the forest floor, gradually swallowing details of trunks and branches, until only the sky remained bright, and the jungle noises – the calls of birds and monkeys – dwindled into silence.

Then a peacock would give an abrupt alarm honk. A muntjac would bark. Some big predator was on its way. Binoculars magnified the last of the daylight, and suddenly the visitor realized, with the hair on his neck rising, that there, right in the middle of his lenses, stood a 500 lb cat. As it turned its head in the direction of the machan, its eyes – the brightest of any animal on earth – caught the last of the western sunset and flashed as bright as halogen lamps.

Not the slightest sound had marked its approach, but when it settled to feed, the cracking of bones rattled out across the water like small-arms fire. Little by little Billy would turn on the lamp, revealing a magnificent male tiger at his dinner, unmoved by the gentle illumination, its orange stripes darkened to deep-brown ochre by the reddish glow from above. After giving his guests a few minutes' spellbound observation, Billy would fade the light again, and the humans would climb silently down from their perch, leaving the king of the jungle to finish his meal in peace.

Comments in the Tiger Haven visitors' book reveal how warmly tourists responded to the special qualities of the place. They were thrilled to escape from the frantically bustling world outside into an oasis of tranquillity, and delighted to find themselves taken into the heart of an Indian family. First to write in the book was Paul Leyhausen, who arrived in January 1974 white and shaken after the journey. When Mira asked him if he would like a bath, he seemed startled and said, 'Why – do I look as though I need one?' Then, and throughout his week-long stay, he declined all offers of a tub, and, with his lengthy, pedantic monologues bored the company to distraction; yet when he left, he wrote a charming tribute: 'I wouldn't know what to praise first. May Tiger Haven live for ever as a memento of what man's greed has destroyed [elsewhere] ... as a joy for all who will come and study or just marvel ... and as a monument to one man's determination, dedication and persistence.'

~

Other comments were shorter but no less enthusiastic. 'I cannot wait to come back and make a film,' wrote Dieter Plage after his first visit in 1975. Elsa M. Sharp of the *Straits Times* in Singapore was 'totally seduced by the environment, the tiger, the leopard, and Billy!' Others wrote, 'A magic connection of mind, heart and soul ... An unbelievably wonderful experience ... My life is refreshed for having been here ... A paradise ... An epoch-making experience ... Three of the happiest days of our lives ... Stellar! ... Should it not be called Tiger Heaven?'

Not the least of the attractions was the food – Indian, of course – for Billy (or Mira) always had excellent cooks, and none more resourceful than Hanif, who remained with the family for more than forty years. A culinary magician, he created sumptuous meals on a dreadful little coal-fired stove: his khir – a form of rice pudding – was so delicious that it made visitors exclaim with delight. Billy himself was, and is, a good trencherman, with the curious habit of mashing all the ingredients of a meal together and eating them with a spoon. He has done this all his life – and when he was a boy, his father once asked if he could not be fed on his own, so disturbing was his performance for everyone else.

Paying tourists apart, members of the family came to stay, as did many friends – and none was more generous to Billy than Haik Sookias, a successful Armenian entrepreneur based partly in Calcutta, where he has his own firm, and partly in the United States. The son of a stockbroker, a self-made man and a very self-sufficient character, Haik first met Balram in Calcutta, and it was through him that he came to Tiger Haven. He knew nothing about animals (and still, according to Billy, knows nothing); but, having felt the magic of the place, and seen what Billy was trying to achieve, he gave unstinting financial support, without which Billy might not have survived.

Another regular visitor was John Withnell, formerly a squadron leader in the Royal Air Force, who shared a chummery, or communal flat, with Balram in Calcutta, and remained a friend for life. Balram's boss Colin Montgomery also came to Tiger Haven many times: another ex-RAF officer, he had been shot down and taken prisoner during World War II.

With memories of the Christmas hunting camps still fresh in their minds, the family would gather at Tiger Haven for seasonal celebrations, here fondly remembered by Billy's cousin Mahindar Singh, who spent much time with the family

Tigers at play: Billy and Tara on the lawns of Tiger Haven

✦ ✦ ✦

(*Photo: Ashish Chandola*)

Billy with the women in his life: Harriet and Juliette

Facing page: (above) Harriet, and (below) Tiffany the Fishing Cat
lands a catch (*Photo: Stanley Breeden*)

♦ ♦ ♦

(*Photos: Courtesy Billy Arjan Singh*)

Standing tall: Billy with Tara,
(*Photo: Lisa van Gruisen*) and
(below) Eelie and young Tara
(*Photo: Courtesy Billy Arjan Singh*)

✦✦✦

Sanctuary for man and beast: Tiger Haven (*Photo: Mike Price*)

Facing page: Cats and dogs:
Eelie and Prince indulge in some good-natured rough and tumble

✦ ✦ ✦

(*Photos: Billy Arjan Singh*)

Honouring the honorary tiger: Billy at 87, receiving the J. Paul Getty
Award for Environment at Dudhwa National Park HQ in 2005

✦ ✦ ✦

(*Photo courtesy: Ravi Singh, World Wildlife Fund*)

as a boy, and, like both their fathers, had been to Balliol College, Oxford:

> We start the morning with a cup of steaming tea and toast, shared with Eelie. After the morning walk, breakfast includes traditional porridge, eggs and bacon and plenty of toast, marmalade and fruit. Elevenses means coffee and cake and beer and gin for the men, continuing until lunch time. In between, for the younger set, there is stump cricket and of course the Pallia Open Golf Championships, played with a couple of rusty clubs, old balls and any amount of holes – the classic upset to form being when a buffalo decides to lie on Balram's ball.
>
> A sumptuous lunch is followed by a much-needed siesta, and then Billy takes a party of visitors to a machan a few hundred yards away, where a tiger has killed a buffalo. As the sun sinks, the jungle springs to life, and across the river a sambhar bellows a sharp alarm call. Old Crooked Foot, the tiger, is on the prowl. For the next half hour we have a thrilling wait, as the jungle animals announce his movements. Finally he passes under our machan and reaches the kill.
>
> Hot baths in large tin tubs, by candlelight, revive us, and a couple of pegs later we gather round the tree covered in decorations, with presents at its base. Carols start the proceedings, and a blazing log fire enables even senior members to recall their old songs, some of them quite bawdy.
>
> Recorded music and an old Hohner squeeze-box keep spirits aglow, and turkey, river fish and lots of goodies add to the enjoyment, until the lights go out and the staff bring in the Christmas pudding, with brandy ablaze.
>
> At the end the men gather round a bush outside, a Balliol man sings *Gordouli*, and all goes well until Tiffany the fishing cat lets out a loud miaow and rasps at the singer's legs, demanding to be fed. *Gordouli* is stopped in mid-stream, and the cat is hastily given bits of fish. Billy solemnly raises his glass in the most poignant of all toasts, "To absent friends" – and so to bed, perhaps to hear the trumpeting of a wild elephant or the roar of a tiger defending his territory.

~

Among the early tourists were the Aspinall family. When their plans for a visit were taking shape, at the end of 1976, John asked if his daughter Amanda, who was then seventeen, might stay on for an indefinite period to gain experience of animals in the wild. Billy agreed, and John and Sally flew out from London in February 1977, bringing Amanda and Sally's friend Arabella Heathcote-Amory with them; and although Billy was acutely aware that his domestic facilities in no way measured up to those of Howletts, the visit proved an enormous success. Aspinall was entranced by Tiger Haven and its semi-resident carnivores, and Billy felt that, given the choice, he would have preferred to live in a natural and fairly primitive environment of this kind, rather than surrounded by the high degree of luxury to which he was accustomed at home.

Aspers, needless to say, startled the rest of the party with a characteristic burst of exhibitionism. When Billy loaded up two cars, to go and spend a night in the forest by the Haunted Pool, at the junction of the Neora and Nagrol rivers, he naturally took the passenger seat in the lead vehicle, leaving Sally to climb into the back, and when they reached their destination, he stripped off all his clothes in front of everyone else, strangers included, to wade naked into the river. Mira was deeply shocked and never forgave him – but as soon as he returned to England, he sent a generous financial contribution, and in thanking him Billy wrote: 'It is good to feel that in this embattled world there are still good friends of animals like you.'

Amanda stayed on at Tiger Haven as planned – and it was Harriet's habit of padding silently around the buildings that led to an unnerving incident. Early one morning the girl accidentally left the door of her room open, and as she sat on her bed, clad only in a towel after a bath, she suddenly felt a huge paw on either shoulder. For a few seconds she was pleased, thinking that Harriet had come to greet her, and she enjoyed the feeling of velvet-soft fur as the leopard pressed its head against her cheek. Then suddenly teeth drove into her neck and claws penetrated the skin on her back. With the loudest possible scream she struggled to her feet and crashed out through the door onto the balcony with Harriet still on her shoulders.

Amar's daughter Priya, who was also staying, rushed to her rescue. So did Billy, who was outside, lifting his weights as usual. Running up the steps, he found Amanda on the floor of the balcony with Harriet on top of her. Grabbing the leopard by the scruff of the neck, he dragged her off, but by then, as he put it, 'her blood was up', and she circled him in a menacing crouch, trying to put in another attack.

Amanda, though shaken, emerged from the encounter unscathed except for a puncture by one ear and some claw-marks on her back. Billy, also, was shaken – more than he cared to admit. His immediate reaction was to send Babu Lal speeding for the doctor, with orders to bring an anti-tetanus jab at once – and when this arrived, the syringe which the medicine man wielded was so huge that Amanda was even more scared of it than of the leopard.

Perhaps to let down his own tension and anxiety, Billy teased her roughly by saying, 'Look here – you've grown up with large animals, and you're at least twenty pounds heavier than Harriet. You shouldn't put up with that sort of thing!' All the same, he acknowledged that 'it had been a nasty moment', and saw that Harriet could be dangerous in certain circumstances. He also wrote a contrite letter to Amanda's father, asking if he would like her to come home; Aspinall characteristically replied that he was happy for her to stay, but in fact she remained at Tiger Haven for only a couple of months, instead of the year which she had planned.

The person who did stay on for nearly a year – and would have liked to be there indefinitely – was Priya, who loved working with animals, and had a natural bent for it. Only her poor sight prevented her: a congenital defect in her eyes had left her with limited vision, and Billy felt this was too much of a handicap in the jungle. She too was nervous of Harriet, who, as she put it, 'kept appearing silently from nowhere', and would lie in wait on a tree by the bridge, to intercept humans when they came in from walks. As a safety measure, Billy made Priya go around equipped with a stick and an old tin can, which she could bang to scare the leopard off. With Tara, in contrast, she felt quite safe. The tigress did sometimes jump up and knock her flat, but she knew that it was only in play. Harriet was different: she seemed to dislike women, and stalked several others besides Priya, among them the wife of the American tiger expert Chuck McDougal. She too had to be rescued by Billy, who dragged Harriet off her.

Priya, who observed the leopard over several months, felt that the animal had become confused by her dual existence: she was never entirely domesticated or entirely wild, but veered between two different environments. Yet Priya understood, as few others did, the intensity of Billy's relationship with Harriet. The leopard, she saw, adored her human partner: their reunions, when Harriet returned to base, were 'incredibly loving'. The leopard would sit down beside Billy and lick the top of his head in ecstasies of affection.

Another visitor that summer was Lisa van Gruisen, a tall and attractive young woman with a powerful personality, who had settled in Kathmandu and was working in Jim Edwards' firm, Mountain Travel. Billy hardly knew whether to be shocked or impressed when she arrived at Tiger Haven with one man, Leo LeBon (President of Mountain Travel, USA), and left with another (Mike Price, the Survival Anglia cameraman); but for ever after – even when she married Tensing Choegyal, a Tibetan nobleman, and settled down with a family – he referred to her as 'the Maneater'. Lisa remained a loyal supporter, and allowed Billy to use a lovely photograph which she took of him playing with Tara as the jacket illustration on the back of his book *Tiger, Tiger*.

TEN

MANEATERS

Devastated though he was by the loss of Harriet and Mameena, Billy at least had the consolation of knowing that Tara was alive and well in the jungle. Having opted for the wild in January 1978, the tigress never consorted with him again. As he searched the forest for her, he fervently hoped that they would meet and exchange courtesies; but though he frequently saw her, she never approached him any more. Once she stood at the Junction Bridge and called to him. Many times she remained standing at a distance and looked at him for longer than a fully wild tiger would have, as though remembering their association, but then she always made herself scarce. Cynical friends remarked that, if the two had met face to face, Billy might not have survived the encounter, and quoted Edward Lear:

> There was a young lady of Riga
> Who went for a ride on a tiger.
> They returned from the ride
> With the lady inside
> And a smile on the face of the tiger.

Instead of fraternizing, Tara moved off, as Billy put it, into 'the world of darkness, those velvet hours between twilight and dawn denied to the human intruder.' Inevitably he was sad that his unique partnership had been broken; but at the same time he derived tremendous satisfaction from the fact that his experiment had worked, and he was content that he had made a significant addition to the stock of Dudhwa tigers, giving it an infusion of entirely fresh genes.

Barely two months passed, however, before a sinister new development took place. On 2 March a cart man named Akbar was killed by a tiger in the area known as the Hulaskhani Bhagar, near Sathiana, on the bank of the Neora river some six miles west of Tiger Haven – and so began a saga of man-killing and maneating which resulted, over the next ten years, in the deaths of nearly 200 humans and thirteen tigers in Kheri alone. From the beginning local people blamed Billy, claiming that the maneater was Tara: her peculiar upbringing had left her unable to hunt wild animals, they said, and robbed her of a normal tiger's fear of humans, so that she had turned on them for prey.

The death of Akbar did not surprise Billy in the least: in fact he had almost predicted it, for the forest had been invaded by a horde of woodcutters and cart drivers who were extracting timber blown down in a storm. This kind of operation had been specifically prohibited by the Wildlife Act of 1972, and Billy had vehemently opposed it; yet in Dudhwa it had been sanctioned by the chairman of the local management committee, with the proviso that the money raised should go to park funds.

In any case, during October 1977 a small army of men had made camp at the edge of the forest, in prime tiger habitat, and they remained there for the next nine months. The operation was supposed to have finished at the end of January 1978, but it dragged on for week after week, as trucks ground about in low gear, the wooden wheels of buffalo carts squealed and the men yelled at the tops of the voices, not just to control their animals, but to give themselves courage in what they reckoned, all too rightly, was a dangerous environment. The smell of unwashed humanity, the noise and general disturbance drove away the local prey species such as deer and pigs, with the result that tigers began to hang about the edges of the encampments. It was there, when Akbar went to answer a call of nature beside a clump of narkul grass, that a tiger got him.

Billy, summoned to the scene early next morning, found the man's lungi, or loincloth, folded on the ground. From this he inferred that Akbar had taken it off to relieve himself – for if it had been pulled off him as he was hauled away, it would have been stretched out along the ground. This in turn meant that the tiger had probably snatched him as he squatted down, for squatting reduces a human to half his or her height, and produces a target more like a monkey than an upright biped, which a tiger would normally avoid.

The body had been dragged about twenty yards, but not eaten, and by the time it was recovered, the tiger had also killed a bullock which had been tethered nearby. Billy at once recognized the pug marks as those of a male, and thought they had been made by the tiger he knew as Long Toes, who had been sharing a range with Tara's Male.

This was the first incident of a man being killed by a tiger in the area for nearly twenty years; but two more fatal attacks took place during the same month of March 1978 and even though they were widely scattered – one ten miles away, the other more than forty – and had been carried out by different tigers, they marked the beginning of what Billy described as 'an endemic conflict between tigers and humans'. The basic cause was an influx of tigers from Nepal, where habitat had been devastated by indiscriminate tree-felling, and in consequence an increasing number of clashes between the two-legged and four-legged species, sometimes inside the forest, as at Hulaskhani Bhagar, but often outside it as well, in the crops of sugar cane which farmers had started planting recklessly close to the edges of the jungle, and in which tigers liked to lie up. (The government had set up four sugar-processing factories in the immediate area, and encouraged farmers to grow cane by making loans available on favourable terms.)

Akbar's death set off an immediate clamour for the tiger to be declared a maneater and shot; but the chief wildlife warden – the only person empowered to issue such a declaration and order – declined to come down from Lucknow, and no action was taken. The outcry gradually died down, but Long Toes (in Billy's view) had done a good job: he had put the wind up the cart men so effectively that they decamped from Hulaskhani and settled below the Dudhwa forest rest house. Even there they did not feel safe for long, and when Tara's Male killed a buffalo near the Twin Lakes, a short distance south-west of Dudhwa, they upped and quit.

The next incident took place at Ambargarh, to the north of Sathiana, near the Nepalese border, a place once deep in the forest, but by then in open farmland, the jungle having been cleared for agriculture. On 3 April a Nepali went into the forest, allegedly to look for cattle, on the Indian side of the frontier, and failed to return home. A search party found his rib cage – all that was left of him – on the bank of the Neora, and brought it home for cremation.

Summoned once more, Billy found that the killing had again been done by a male tiger, accompanied by a tigress with two young cubs. Again there was an outcry, and again no action was taken; but within three days, on 6 April, the tiger struck once more. As before, the victim had gone off into the jungle on his own, illegally, and when a search party (which included the park director, R.L. Singh, and some armed guards) went to look for him next morning, they came on a male tiger eating his remains. Even though they shouted at him, and pelted him with branches, he dragged the remains of the body off into cover. The park director had clearly seen that the killer was a male, but no matter: he blandly announced that the culprit was Tara.

When Billy went to the site with Jackson, they found that the tigress with cubs had again been present – so whichever animal had made the kill, the mother had eaten from it as well. Obviously, in the absence of normal prey, the father was killing humans to feed his family. Billy was infuriated to hear R.L. Singh say that, if he had had the authority, he would have shot the tiger himself. Rather than take account of the peculiar circumstances which had made the animal turn on humans, or work out some way of saving it, he would simply have written it off.

To Billy, the obvious way of tiding the family over was to stake out buffalo baits in their area, and he suggested as much. But before anything had been done, there was another fatality. This time a Tharu tribal, reputed to have been simple-minded, wandered into the jungle on 27 April at Kiratpur, two miles west of the most recent incident. Yet again Billy took Jackson with him to investigate: they went to the spot where the man had been seized and followed the drag, back and forth across the bed of the Neora, which was then dry. The pug marks were those of a male. Then:

Presently, beneath a bush, we found an arm, and a patch of blood where the body had been eaten during the night. From there, I was surprised to see, a tigress had taken over the drag. Following up further, I found the pug marks of a small cub in the sand on another bend of the river – and there, with features set in a hideous grin of death, was the tonsured head of the victim, cleaned of all hair by the tigress's rasping tongue.

To Billy's intense relief, R.L. Singh belatedly accepted his advice and arranged to have baits put out. For the next six weeks the local tigers dined largely on buffalo, and attacks on humans ceased: the maneater had evidently changed his ways. Although, as Billy recorded, 'official accounts of the episode never admitted any such heresy'. Between and after the various alarms, he continued his normal patrols in search of information, his particular aim at that stage being to obtain photographs of Tara which would indisputably prove she was living wild on the range. Several times he came on a big male tiger cooling off in the river. At first the animal bolted when it saw him, but soon it got so used to him that it would remain in the water, immersed to the eyebrows.

Trouble broke out again in August, when a man was taken on farmland immediately outside the park, and his body was found partly eaten. Dogs and chickens began to disappear. A few days later, another man was killed: like the first, he had been working close to a stand of sugar cane. From its pug marks, the marauder was reckoned (though not by Billy) to be a tigress, and for once the authorities agreed that they should try to anaesthetize the animal with a tranquillizing dart, rather than eliminate her. The attempt at immobilization was, in Billy's phrase, 'a Gilbertian affair', with an untrained wildlife warden dutifully firing off his single dart at a distance of about 150 yards, when the maximum effective range was forty.

In the event, a farmer sitting on the machan with him shot the killer dead with an unlicensed rifle. When it turned out to be a young male, in perfect condition, the fact that the tracks had been diagnosed as those of a female was quickly forgotten, and the dead tiger was pronounced to be the very one which had wrought havoc at Sathiana and Ambargarh in the spring. In fact it was very much smaller and younger, but, as Billy remarked, 'Government statistics had to be kept up, (and) the easiest thing to do was to tidy up the books by entering the shot animal as the Sathiana maneater – for dead tigers tell no more tales than live ones.'

With logic and truth playing little part in the debate, the clamour for Tara's blood intensified – even though of her twenty-two alleged victims, eight had been killed by male tigers, and six by animals of unspecified gender. Nobody was more vociferous in calling for her extinction than 'Tootoo' Imam, a shikar outfitter from Bihar whose business had been undermined by the ban on tiger shooting. Scenting a new possibility, he visited Dudhwa, claimed that Tara had been responsible for nearly thirty kills, and announced that he had one foreign client willing to pay two lakh rupees for the privilege of shooting her. He also wrote an immensely long letter to Jagjivan Ram, the deputy prime minister, with twenty-one copies to various other senior officials, in which he called Billy 'a well-known wildlife enthusiast, fanatic would be a better word', described the letting-loose of Prince as 'a rash and negligent act involving criminal responsibility', and damned the release of Tara as 'an outrage'.

Of course Billy was incensed by irresponsible ranting of this kind, and in an effort to establish a more sensible approach to the problem he invited H.M. Patel, Chairman of the Indian Board for Wildlife, to visit Dudhwa and make his own assessment. On 10 March 1979 Patel flew to Pallia by helicopter, hoping to see Tara for himself. Unfortunately for him, the tigress did not come to the bait that Billy had put out, and the considerable expense of the operation was largely wasted; but the upshot was that the government appointed a committee – of which Billy was not invited to be a member – to investigate the maneating problem and suggest a remedy, and on 21 May they sent down a team of specialists, headed by S.R. Chowdhury, Field Director of the Simlipal Reserve.

Chowdhury was regarded as a leading expert, because for nearly five years he had owned a tame tigress called Khairi, which he kept in an enclosure and took for walks on a lead. He repeatedly said that he was going to return her to the wild, but never did so, and Billy was deeply sceptical about his intentions. Chowdhury, he felt sure, got so much publicity from the animal, and built up his own ego so much by parading it about, that he had no intention of letting it go. In Billy's view the tigress 'remained a house pet, imprinted on her human captors, and subjected to meaningless, pseudo-scientific observation.' He believed that she must have been given birth-control pills, which suppressed her oestrus – otherwise, like Tara, she would have become uncontrollable in her desire to take to the jungle. Nor was Billy impressed by Chowdhury's boast that he personally had shot more than fifty maneaters.

When his report came out, it did admit that the habitat around Dudhwa had been seriously degraded, and that prey species had been reduced to very low levels; it also exonerated Tara, by recording that all the maneaters shot to date had been males. Yet it recommended that the 'socio-ecological conflict' between the tigers and the local population should be solved by the swift removal of any troublesome carnivores, even if that meant killing the wrong animal, and included the gratuitous comment that Tara had 'apparently been naturally eliminated'.

Another of Chowdhury's suggestions was that maneaters might be captured rather than shot. Billy himself advocated capture – but only if the aim was to release the captive in a more suitable area. What he could not endorse was the idea that trapped animals should be put in zoos, for his experience had shown that any tiger which had lived in the wild would only pine and die if put behind bars.

~

In the summer of 1979 Tiger Haven gained a new recruit. After a grass fire at a place called Bellraien, about twenty miles from the farm, a small, spotted cat was found abandoned, and the forest staff were ignorant enough to believe that it was a baby leopard. In trying to feed the little creature, they almost drowned it by pouring milk over its head. Billy, who happened to be in the area, saw at once that it was the kitten of a fishing cat – a separate species about twice the size of a domestic cat – and he took it home to see if he could rear it.

From the start the kitten grew well on buffalo milk fed to her from a dropper; but her good start in life was probably due almost as much to the moral support given her by Eelie, who adopted her as if she was a puppy, licking her clean and allowing her to mountaineer all over her body. Billy named the cat Tiffany, and he was becoming very fond of her when one day, after about a month, she vanished: nobody could find her until Eelie led the way to the edge of the river under the Junction Bridge, and there she was, dabbling for fish with her tiny paws. Billy was amazed, but also thrilled, to see instinct working in this minute creature as surely as it had in Prince and Tara: just as leopard and tiger had taken to their own kind in the forest, so the fishing cat's genes had sent it to the water to search for food.

As she grew up, fishing became her one great skill. Her forelegs were so short that she soon tired on walks, and she was a poor climber, because her tail was not long enough to balance her properly; but whenever she came to a stream, she would take up station at its edge and hook out fish with amazing dexterity.

At night she slept in one of the rooms, but otherwise she was not restrained in any way, and when she was about a year old she mated with a large wild male – a union which produced a single kitten. Thereafter Tiffany took mainly to the wild, but she often returned to the farm, and would peer into Billy's room at first light, calling piteously until he fed her. A year later she gave birth to twins, and proved herself a 'true cat of two worlds' by continuing to make return visits, even though her new kittens remained stand-offish. Finally in March 1984 she was clearly pregnant again, and when she did not appear for three days, Billy deduced that she had produced her third litter in a stand of long grass; but then, at midnight on the 18th, a single loud squawk from the direction of the grass betrayed the fact that a tiger had put in an attack. Two days later descending vultures drew Billy to the remains of a large fishing cat, bigger than Tiffany, which he surmised had been the father, trying to defend his offspring. He could not tell exactly what had happened, but tracks led him to suspect that the culprit was Tara, and that she had killed the fishing cat to protect a young cub of her own. Tiffany disappeared, never to be seen again, and the best he could hope was that she had decamped to a safer area.

~

Billy became enmeshed in still deeper trouble when the tigress he knew as the Median turned on humans. The story of her demise, already told in chapter one, can be briefly recapitulated here. She made her first human kill on 12 January 1980, and accounted for three more deaths (including that of Billy's assistant tracker Lallu) before she was shot by R.L. Singh in November. The reign of terror which she created was relatively brief, but the behaviour of R.L. Singh, who mendaciously claimed for ever afterwards that he had eliminated Tara, poisoned Billy's relationship with the forest service.

Meanwhile, as enemies sniped at him from close at hand, accolades continued to roll in from farther afield. In July 1978 the Dutch ambassador in Delhi staged a cocktail party and ceremony specially for him at the embassy, and, on behalf of Prince Bernhard, presented him with the award of the Golden Ark for general services to wildlife. The Dutch also invited him to go to Holland, but he declined.

A suggestion from Nalini Jayal, in Delhi, that Tara should be fitted with a radio collar had already drowned in the marshes of bureaucracy. The idea had been put up at the end of 1978, when she was still frequenting the neighbourhood of Tiger Haven, and it might then have been possible to tranquillize her with a dart-gun and fit a collar. The technique was being used successfully over the border in Nepal by experts from the Smithsonian Institution in Washington, but when Billy tried to pursue the idea and invite them to Dudhwa, he was blocked by a characteristically futile letter from R.L. Singh:

> I have not received clearance from the Chief Wildlife Warden U.P., hence you cannot be allowed to invite anybody to radio-collar any tiger/tigress in the name of Tara. Please obtain clearance from the Chief Wildlife Warden U.P. before carrying

out any experiment on park animals, otherwise you will be held responsible for violating the park rules.

Becoming positively obstructive, Singh issued verbal orders to his forest guards that if outsiders with radio-tracking equipment made any attempt to enter the area, they were to be arrested.

After babus, Billy's most persistent problem was lack of money, and he had a worrying moment in April 1979, when Grzimek wrote to say that he would be unable to finance the next three years of the experiment, as all his funds were needed to fight well-organized poaching in East Africa. Later he rescinded this decision, even though he was attacked by German specialists who claimed that Tara was not a pure-bred Bengal tigress, and that he should not be supporting her.

By then Mrs Gandhi was out of power, but she kept in touch with Billy, and wrote saying she would like to be more involved with wildlife. 'As you know, I have felt close to animals and nature since childhood, and so have my sons.' In the autumn of 1979 she wrote again: 'No, I have not forgotten the importance of wildlife. But what can I do right now? Please keep in touch with my daughter-in-law Maneka, who is deeply interested in the subject.' In November 1979, after Billy had nerved himself to ask her to stay, she told him, 'Tiger Haven is very tempting, but I do not know when I can come.'

As if the maneater problem were not enough to occupy him, attacks began coming in from an entirely different angle, as people revived the suggestion that Tara was not a pure-bred Bengal tiger, but had alien genes in her ancestry, and accused Billy of introducing a genetic cocktail into the Indian jungle. Most of the insinuations emanated not from close at hand, but from overseas: the ripples started by Tara were spreading out across the world.

By now Billy knew that the international attempt to have her eliminated was being led by Leyhausen, (who had been to Tiger Haven at his own invitation). Billy was not impressed, remarking that 'it seemed ironic that Leyhausen, who now proclaimed the need to maintain genetic purity, had also laid down that the minimum number of tigers needed to maintain genetic diversity in any self-contained pool was no fewer than 300.' As Leyhausen well knew, none of the Indian parks was big enough to accommodate anything like this number – so that he was in effect saying that every group in the Project Tiger reserves was condemned to slow extinction by inbreeding. In Dudhwa, which contained fifty tigers at the most, the population was – by his account – hopelessly small, and would die out in a few generations.

Early in 1980 a German journalist, Wolfgang Frey, wrote to Molly Badham at Twycross asking for information about Tara's background, and in March she replied: 'We do not know the ancestry of the grandparents of the tigress. The parents are Sire Sultan, who came from Aspinall aged three months. The dam was Begum, who came from Edinburgh in approximately 1969.'

Frey also wrote to Billy, saying that he could not imagine that 'such a distinguished conservationist like you will allow any deterioration of the local population of tigers'. Not content with the information from Twycross, the hounds pursued the trail to Scotland, whence Dr Miranda F. Stevenson, Curator of the Royal Zoological Society of Scotland, wrote to H.S. Panwar, Director of Project Tiger:

> Begum was born in Edinburgh Zoo on 4.12.69 to the female Ranee and male Rajah ... Ranee came to us in 1964 and was purchased from Van den Brink, Holland. Reputed to have been born captive in Nepal's zoo ...Rajah came to us from Hagenbeck,

Hamburg. It is possible that the animals are not pure Bengal stock, but we never claimed they were.

~

In September 1980 Billy was dismayed to receive a letter from Peter Scott, the distinguished conservationist who had founded a wildfowl centre of international importance at Slimbridge, on the Severn, near Bristol. In his capacity as Chairman of the Survival Service Commission (part of the IUCN), Scott wrote:

> We understand that the tigress in question is already a hybrid between two races of tiger, neither of them the same as the population in the Dudhwa National Park. If she breeds, it will make a further genetic cocktail, and from a scientific and conservationist point of view this would be deplorable ... Could you confirm that this will not be allowed to happen?

Of course Billy could confirm no such thing. On the contrary, he was determined that Tara should breed. The answer he sent back was a model of restraint – 'I fear it would not be possible to confirm that she will not breed. I do feel that scientific opinion is somewhat strait-laced in its insistence on the purity of the species' – but privately he was incensed that Scott, whom he knew quite well, should have come out on the side of the opposition. Only later did he discover that he had been asked to write the letter by Leyhausen – and he was delighted to hear that, 'having given this extra stir to the storm in the gene cup, the fearless Cat Chairman resigned'.

On 5 October 1981 Panwar wrote to say that he had received 'a volley of correspondence, mostly from persons connected with zoos in Europe', alleging that Tara was not a pedigree Bengal tigress:

It will be a catastrophe of the highest order genetically if our breed of tigers is contaminated by one of impure lineage. Nobody should be more concerned about this than you, whose body and soul have gone into the making of Dudhwa. We must consider her elimination before she breeds. Needless to say, our image as conservationists is coming to be maligned.

Billy remained immoveable. He told Leyhausen that he had no locus standi when it came to mixing genes, because he, a German, had already mixed them by marrying a British wife; and he blew Panwar backwards with a blast of neat sarcasm:

In view of the claim of the Director of the Dudhwa National Park (R.L. Singh) that Tara has already been destroyed, your statement is academic ... I must ask you, however, to let me know the relevant portion of the Indian Wildlife Act which empowers you to (authorize) such destruction ... You can rely on me to resist such a consummation by all legitimate means within my understanding.

This clearly gave Panwar a jolt. 'I am shocked and pained by your reply of 20 October about the doubtful lineage of Tara,' he wrote; and when he came to compile the progress report of Project Tiger for the year 1980-81 (which he completed in May 1982), he abandoned fact altogether:

The Committee have come to the conclusion that Shri Arjan Singh's claim that he was able to rehabilitate the tigress into the wild was untenable. The tigress identified by him as the rehabilitated Tara was in fact a tigress of Dudhwa National Park ... This latter tigress – not Tara, of which there was no trace – was most likely the tigress that was shot by the Park Director.

Panwar was quite shameless about shifting his ground. First he said that Tara must be eliminated, then that she did not exist. Obviously he was trying to create the impression that no genetic cocktail had been let loose, and to defend himself against possible accusations of laxness on his own part.

The truth, as even the most bureaucratic of the babus must have realized, was that no outsider had the slightest chance of finding or identifying Tara in her jungle fastness. They had no clear idea of what she looked like – and in any case, in the dense vegetation of the forest one tigress closely resembles another. Unless they came and massacred all the tigers in Dudhwa – which was clearly not an option in political terms, still less a practical possibility – they could not get rid of her. Even if Billy himself had wanted to remove her, he would have found the task exceedingly difficult. He might conceivably have been able to lure her to a baiting site, and then (if the equipment were available) to dart her; but as things were, he was prepared to go to any length to block attempts on her life or freedom.

In frustration his critics fell back on the argument that he had carried out the whole experiment unilaterally and unofficially, ignoring the fact – of which he kept reminding them – that Tara's importation had been sanctioned by the prime minister of the day. Billy felt certain that his critics were being driven by jealousy: Panwar and others had claimed that it was impossible to introduce a super-predator to the wild, and he had proved them wrong. 'Their whole aim,' he reflected later, 'was to knock me off my perch.'

In February 1981, at a meeting of the Indian Board for Wildlife, chaired by Mrs Gandhi, he suggested that a special body should be created to investigate causes of the man-eating, which had already accounted for sixty deaths in Dudhwa. A committee was appointed, with Panwar as secretary, but since one of its mandates was to report on the feasibility of introducing hand-reared predators to the wild, Billy was naturally excluded, and at no stage of their inquiries did members seek his views or ask for any of the abundant evidence that he could have given them.

The committee's report, published a year later, agreed that the main reason for the maneating was the pressure of human population on areas of tiger habitat, but of the various remedial measures proposed, only one was implemented. This was that compensation should be paid for the deaths of humans and cattle; but the amounts were derisory – only Rs 5,000 for a human life – and the others were too ambitious to be tackled. One suggested the creation of Tiger Watch teams in every Project Tiger area, which would monitor the movements of suspected maneaters and remove 'proven aberrants'; another, that a far larger reserve should be created around Dudhwa, with long forest corridors linking the existing jungle to the two other core areas of Kishanpur and Pilibhit – a project which would have meant the relocation of several entire villages. Drastic measures of this kind had already been taken to improve the park at Ranthambore, but at Dudhwa they were never seriously contemplated.

To Billy, the whole episode symbolized what had gone wrong with the management of wildlife in India:

> Instead of accepting what I had done in a practical and creative spirit, the officials of Project Tiger were driven by their own scientific dogma – perhaps also by baser influences such as jealousy – to refute the existence of a unique animal, to deny that anything had been achieved at all, and to erect in their defence a tissue of counter-claims about as strong as a spider's web.

~

The worst problem, at grassroots level, was that measures to protect tigers carried no votes for politicians. Subsistence farmers naturally resisted the idea of any scheme which would prevent them from growing sugar cane – and indeed, with the connivance of corrupt forest officials, they were continually encroaching on the jungle, digging up boundary pillars, moving them a hundred yards or so into the forest and felling the trees left outside the new border, all to create new fields and living-space. As Billy ruefully remarked, 'Corruption is everywhere. Everything has a price.'

Although he hated the way in which immigrants piled into the area looking for land, he was by no means unsympathetic to the problems of established villagers. He knew perfectly well that if they lost crops to deer and pigs, or had a ploughing buffalo taken by a tiger, they usually had no option but to go to the local money-lender for a loan and interest rates were so scandalously high – up to seventy per cent per annum – that a borrower had no hope of clearing a debt in his own lifetime. Such men obviously could not be expected to subscribe to the conservation of wildlife for aesthetic reasons.

The first necessity, Billy saw, was a fence to keep wild animals out of cultivated areas, and the second, a fund to compensate for losses. But the only long-term solution was to make the inhabitants of villages bordering on the park see that wildlife could be a direct benefit to them, because it could attract wealthy tourists, who would spend money in the area – a concept successfully put into practice in and around the Corbett National Park.

By the autumn of 1981 echoes of the gene row had become public as far afield as Germany. 'Newspapers report that the tiger given by us has killed people,' said a telegram from Grzimek. 'Please wire facts.' In a letter of 2 November he wrote:

> In our newspapers was published that the tigress Tara donated by us is a maneater now and has killed or hurt eighty humans. It should therefore be killed. Of course such nonsense makes it difficult for us to collect money for conservation in this country.

~

In February 1982 Billy received some much-needed moral support from John Aspinall, who came out with Sally and again stayed at Tiger Haven. In a letter dated 24 March, which he obviously meant Billy to show around as he liked, Aspers wrote:

> As the breeder of over 250 tigers in the past twenty years ... I can throw some light on Tara's paternal grandparents, who were the first tigers to arrive at Howletts in 1958. Her grand-dam, also called Tara, came from Edinburgh Zoo, and she showed none of the typical signs which suggest South-east Asian origin. I procured her mate Mazar from an Austrian zoo ... his markings suggest that his ancestors must have emanated from Malaya or Sumatra.
>
> The point to remember is that all tigers are closely related ... (This is) a storm in a gene cup. Practical men in the field like yourself must try and ignore the well-meant but irrelevant bickerings of academics and armchair pundits, whose coccyxes are under continual strain from sitting on committees. If the remaining wild animals of India could choose their own pantheon, I have little doubt you would have a high and honoured place there.

Generous as ever, John sent Billy £1,000 with which to buy a new elephant (Sitara having died suddenly, apparently of a heart attack). But the Dudhwa authorities, blinkered as always, told him that if he got one, it would not be allowed into the park – even though they had a few working elephants of their own – and so he never went through with the purchase.

Another welcome supporter was Prince Philip, Duke of Edinburgh. Writing as President of the World Wildlife Fund in December 1982, the Duke said:

> I hear from all sides nothing but admiration for what you have achieved for conservation in India, and I can only say I am sorry if you have run into difficulties. The trustees of the World Wildlife Fund are naturally interested in the problem of the maneating tigers in India.

~

When the Duke accompanied the Queen on a visit to India in November 1983, he invited Billy to a reception at the British High Commission in Delhi, where the two had an agreeable chat, and Prince Philip got a firsthand account of the Ghola maneater, which had created havoc almost at the doorstep of Tiger Haven earlier that year.

The first two attacks had come in May 1983, in farmland just outside the park, opposite Sathiana – the very area from which Billy and George Schaller had once herded the swamp deer. Twice the same man was seized by a tiger – once at night, and once in daylight – and twice, by amazing luck, he escaped. But then, in quick succession, the marauder killed a girl outside her hut and a cultivator who was levelling his field for sowing.

By what Billy called 'some peculiar process of deduction' the forest department decided that the killer was a female, and baited cage traps were set out in patches of sugar cane. When Billy went to look round the area, he found the pug marks of no fewer than four different tigers, two of them males: clearly

174 | HONORARY TIGER

a whole family was involved. Inevitably, one of them went into a cage at night and was caught; but because the only man capable of tranquillizing the captive was out of the area, he did not reach the scene until 3 p.m. the next afternoon. By then some 10,000 people had streamed out of Pallia and the surrounding villages, walking three or four miles to stare at the monster, and the tiger had sustained numerous injuries in its attempts to escape. When the research officer at last managed to knock it out, he took its temperature by lifting its tail and inserting a thermometer into its anus – and after a close-up inspection he pronounced the animal to be a male.

As Billy later remarked, a tiger's sexual organs are so prominent that it seemed scarcely possible that the research officer made a mistake. Nevertheless, when the animal arrived in Lucknow, the zoo authorities announced that it was a female, and they stuck to this fiction to the bitter end. Billy was enraged by such dishonesty, and by the authorities' craven attempt to appease local fear and anger. The forest department, he wrote:

> ... had condemned an innocent animal to penal servitude and a slow death. In order to maintain the charade, they placed the "tigress" behind a screen, away from public gaze, on the spurious excuse that "she" was upset by being stared at. The next development was the announcement that "she" had died of snakebite – in a concrete cage. A disgraceful and shameful episode in wildlife conservation was officially closed.

~

At Ghola – needless to say – the killings continued. Late one afternoon a tiger snatched another man as he squatted to urinate beside a stand of sugar cane, and dragged him into the crop. Friends set fire to the cane in an attempt to scare the tiger off, but when they drove a tractor into the devastated field, they found only a dead body.

When Billy reached the scene next morning, he was surrounded by a mob of women screaming for his blood. The killer, they shrieked, was Tara. It was he who had started the whole reign of terror by letting her loose in the park. The maneater must be shot immediately. In vain Billy pointed out that the pug marks were clearly those of a male. He told the people that they had no right to be living where they were, and when they tried to justify their presence by saying they had occupied the area for ten years, he did nothing to calm them by telling them that tigers had lived there for over a thousand.

Next morning the tiger killed again, seizing a girl from outside her hut, a mile away, and yet another death came a few days later, when a man who had been levelling his field for sowing was grabbed and dragged into a stand of cane. Goaded by fear, the locals set up such agitation that the villain, described as a tigress in spite of Billy's identification of the tracks, was officially declared a maneater, and the new park director, Ashok Singh, was detailed to destroy it.

He therefore had a machan built and sat up over a small, tethered buffalo; but due to various bungles, and one botched shot, the tiger managed to eat most of the bait and drag the rest away. Locals now began to claim that they were haunted by the malevolent spirit of a farmer, killed in a dispute years earlier, which had now taken up residence in the body of the maneater, and could not be destroyed. That night Ashok Singh again sat up over a bait. Once more the tiger came, and he took a hurried shot at it, without any definite result.

In the morning he was so flustered that he came looking for Billy and asked him to take charge of the hunt. At the scene, recriminations flew, until Jackson found a smear of blood, which showed that the tiger had been wounded and had gone to lie up in the sugar cane. Because it was too dangerous to enter the dense cane on foot, Billy assembled four elephants, which began to comb through the field, until a harsh snarl erupted from almost under one of the trampling beasts. Evidence that the tiger was far from dead scattered the searchers: some edged away, but Billy insisted that they should close in and finish the wounded animal off.

A man called Kulminder Singh (known as 'Kinda'), who had a farm beside the Soheli only two miles from Tiger Haven, suggested that a tractor towing a levelling-plank should open up lanes through the cane, to improve visibility. After a two-hour wait, a machine arrived and started work – but hardly had it begun when the owner of the field also arrived, and objected strenuously to the destruction of his crop. The rest of the story is best told in Billy's own words:

> Soon temperaments flared: the owner of the field slapped the tractor-driver. The tractor-owner took umbrage and fired a smooth-bore shot at the farmer, although fortunately from a distance. For a while a fight between two factions of the Sikh community seemed imminent. No sooner had peace been restored than local settlers attacked the Sikh armed with sticks and stones for not letting his field be levelled. When he leapt into jeep and drove off, they brought matters to a head by setting fire to the crop.
>
> As the vaulting flames leapt through the cane, the tiger was seen limping slowly and painfully across one of the lanes, and it became clear that he would not leave cover until he had to ... Sensing what the end would be, everyone who was armed dismounted, except for the Park Director, and formed a line across the north-eastern end of the field, where the blaze was obviously going to burn out.

The firing squad's formidable armament included three .375 magnum rifles, one .30-06, two .315s and an assortment of smooth bores. The marksmen formed the front line, and immediately behind them about 200 local inhabitants waited eagerly for the grand finale.

As the flames approached, the heat became intense, even where we stood, away from the edge of the crop. In the end only one small triangular patch remained unburnt ... and at last (the tiger) emerged in front of us with a defiant snarl. At the first two shots he buckled and went down. Then he staggered to his feet again, but when I fired he crumpled and collapsed. A great cheer rent the air, and everyone began firing wildly in a *feu de joie*.

The women who had previously threatened to assault me now hastened to garland me with tinsel, crying out "Arjan Singh ki jai!" – "Praise be to Arjan Singh!" Their sudden and violent change of mood reflected all too clearly the state of terror to which the maneater had reduced them.

As Billy had predicted, the killer turned out to be a male, in his prime. Under his skin were several charges of buckshot, but the pellets were healed over, and had not been inhibiting his movements. There was no major physical deformity to account for his attacks on humans: his sole reason for turning on them was that the territories of the species had overlapped.

The Ghola incident had a vicious aftermath, when armed Sikh terrorists, in search of land, came to Kulminder Singh and demanded shelter. At first Kinda took up with them, and helped them establish a camp inside the national park. Then he turned informer and led the constabulary to their hideout – only for the police to turn tail and run after an exchange of gunfire.

A few nights later, at 3 a.m., seven Sikhs armed with AK-47 rifles arrived at the farm of Kinda's neighbour Tarsem Singh Musafir. They took Tarsem to Kinda's house and made him call out: when Kinda appeared, a heated argument broke out, and they shot him – as they did his wife, when she came out. They then poured diesel oil on the bodies, set them and the house alight, and departed, leaving a note to say that this was the reward for betrayal

It was suspected that the instigator of the murders was the Sikh whose cane field had been levelled and burnt during the hunt at Ghola. Some months later a terrorist arrested in south India confessed to the crime, but by then the police had decided that the only effective cure in such feuds was a bullet for a bullet, so they did not book the prisoner under the appropriate section of the penal code, but took him to a lonely grove in the early hours and shot him out of hand.

Such was the havoc that a single maneater could cause. Again and again Billy argued that the only way for men and tigers to coexist in amity was for them to live apart, and he advocated numerous measures to achieve such a separation. One was that a five-mile wide buffer zone, free of sugar cane, should be established round the park. In that area farmers would be paid not to grow cane, but would be encouraged to plant short crops such as wheat and barley which gave tigers no cover. He also called for an electric fence to be established round the boundary of the park, to keep predators and prey species inside. Further, he suggested that people living near the park should be given financial help to build proper houses, rather than grass huts, and provided with bio-gas cookers fuelled by methane – two measures which would drastically reduce the huge annual demand for natural building materials and firewood which was drawing thousands of locals into the park every winter.

In between all the maneater alarms, he devoted countless hours to monitoring Tara's movements about the jungle, and in trying to get good photographs of her – something which he eventually managed, with the help of a remotely-controlled flash gun, when she came to a baiting site that he had created specially for her. By May 1981, when she was five years old, he was becoming worried that she had not yet produced cubs; but then, on 7, 8 and 9 May, his persistent reconnaissance was rewarded, and he watched spellbound from hides on the river bank as Tara and her big male mated repeatedly on sand-spits beside the water. Those days, he reckoned, were some of the most fascinating and rewarding he had ever spent in the jungle; and Mira, who joined him to observe some of the action, was amazed by the hollow growls that Tara kept giving – a sound so strange that she thought it was a motor boat coming up the river.

Knowing that a zoo tigress' normal term of pregnancy is 105 days, Billy looked forward to 21 August, and the days that succeeded it, with intense anticipation; but although on that day Tara was moving around her normal area, and regularly killing baits, she gave no sign that she had had cubs until Day 118 – the 4th of September – when she changed her routine, making Billy suspect that she had a family and, for security, had shifted it to a new base.

At that point he had to leave for a trip to England, and when he returned six weeks later Jackson had no definite news for him. It was not until early February 1982 that he at last found evidence, in the form of pug marks, that Tara had at least two cubs. They must, by then, have been five months old, and the fact that searching humans had found no trace of them was a tribute to the skill with which their mother had kept them hidden.

Billy's first sighting of them came one morning in the middle of February, when he walked out to a hide on the river bank, peered through a hole in the screen and found Tara gazing straight at him from a sand-spit. A moment later two cubs walked out into the open, but a warning growl from their mother put them straight back into cover. Soon after that he found the tracks of a third cub, and during a night of bright moonlight spent on the Double-storey Machan, he saw all three playing on the sand and heard them splashing in the shallows. At first light he came down, with the intention of relieving himself, when suddenly two of the cubs rushed into view, chasing each other, within ten yards of where he was standing. 'Both parties stared at each other,' he recorded, 'the cubs sitting on their hunkers with expressions of amazement on their little faces at finding they were not alone on the sandbank.'

Realizing that Tara must be somewhere very close, Billy went back up the machan for a few minutes, until Jackson came out to join him, and then set off for home, walking silently along the path that followed the river. When he again heard splashes on his left, he crept up to vantage point:

> I beheld an enchanting sight – all three cubs playing in the river. Two solemnly sat in the water, immersed up to their small heads, while the third kept scrambling on to a horizontal log, whence it would leap back into the stream ... Now, as I watched fascinated, a movement farther up the river caught my eye. There on the bank sat the mother, anxiously watching her offspring from a patch of bracken. Soon, inevitably, she caught sight of us and stood up to roar defiance at the intruders on the family scene. Explosive bursts of noise echoed through the tall trees. At once the gambolling cubs knew that something was wrong and scampered off into the jungle, water spraying from their coats.

Even that thrilling experience paled before another which Billy

got a few days later, when he went out at first light to check
the bait at the Spillway Machan:

> When I looked through the screen, I saw Tara standing next to
> the dead buffalo, growling softly, with her gaze fixed on the
> machan. Through my binoculars I had a wonderful view of her:
> with absolute clarity I made out the inverted catapult of stripes
> on her left cheek, her characteristic eye-spot. I thought she had
> never looked so beautiful.
>
> I was seized by an almost-overwhelming desire to go and
> stroke her; to tell her that I wished her family no harm; to say
> that although she had left me for her own kind and a better
> world, I still loved her and wished her well. But she, indifferent
> to my telepathic messages, soon moved off and sat down behind
> the Spillway, where a cub came and massaged its back against
> her chin.

~

Insatiable in his desire to gather insights into tiger behaviour,
Billy continued to patrol the jungle by day and sit up over baits
at night. One of his most rewarding observations came on a
night when Tara's Male began to feed on a buffalo at the site
opposite the Double-storey Machan, clearly visible under the
glow of the red lamp. Out of the darkness behind him
materialized one of the cubs, the weakling of the three, which
Billy had feared was ill or physically retarded. The scrawny
teenager lay down and waited, front paws together, at a
respectful distance, until her father had eaten his fill. Then he
got up, turned to her briefly as if to say, 'Your turn now,' and
disappeared into the dark. Billy was enchanted by this
evidence of paternal solicitude:

> Where was the "ineffable malignity" of the Victorian writers?
> Where was the "embodiment of devilish cruelty"? With that one
> charming display of manners, Tara's Male showed what calumny
> had been levelled against his kind.

~

From all his observations over kills, he concluded that unlike lions, which live in essentially competitive prides, tigers are guided by truly parental instincts, and that a father, far from being a menace to his own offspring, as other writers claim, is extremely solicitous, even to the point of allowing his cubs to feed alongside him. Billy found, on the other hand, that adult tigers never feed together, but take turns on a kill, with a strict protocol based on recognition of each other's need for space.

~

Billy's literary affairs, meanwhile, had progressed by fits and starts. He had, at last, acquired a portable typewriter, on which he clattered away; but it was an old model, and at Tiger Haven ribbons were hard to come by. So was maintenance: in the high humidity, parts quickly rusted and jammed, and the lower-case letters became so clogged with dirt that they ceased to register, forcing the operator to use capitals only. But at least Billy could claim that he typed with two fingers, whereas Balram never progressed beyond one.

Having put aside his account of Prince, which Collins had rejected, he had started another book – the story of Tara – and through the agency of his friend Sarah Giles (whose father Frank was editor of *The Sunday Times*) he made contact with Naim Attallah, the proprietor of Quartet Books. When he met Attallah in London, he found him humourless, and had difficulty in agreeing on what was wanted, so that the encounter became rather difficult. Nevertheless, Attallah agreed to bring the book out, and Johnny Moorehead was once again recruited to knock it into shape.

The resulting publication was rather garish, and – as Billy

was the first to admit – premature, for in 1981 the saga of Tara was by no means over. On the contrary, her future looked uncertain, and his main reason for going ahead with the book so quickly was that he felt he needed to stand up for himself by publishing an account of how Tara had come to be where she was. Also, he thought that some of the forest officers might be impressed by the fact that the book had appeared in England, and might therefore become more sympathetic.

By then Survival Anglia's leopard film had been completed, and Billy had expanded his account of Prince to include the story of Harriet and her cubs. He felt that, with the excellent extra material, Collins would have taken it after all. But in the meantime Survival had started trying to buy another publishing house, Allen & Unwin, who said they would be delighted to bring the book out. Then that deal fell through, leaving Billy stranded.

It was through Sarah Giles that he made contact with Tom Maschler, Editorial Director of Jonathan Cape. When Sarah told Tom about Tiger Haven, he decided on impulse to go there; he found it a magical place, and never forgot the thrill of wandering about in the jungle, with Billy unarmed except for his stick. 'To walk about with tigers all round you – it was unheard-of,' he remembered. Cape eventually published the leopard book in 1982 under the title *Prince of Cats,* illustrated with fine photographs by Dieter and Mary Plage and Mike Price, and with some of the author's own.

The book received some respectful reviews: the *Glasgow Herald* called it 'eminently readable', and the *Oxford Times* declared it 'an extraordinary tale'. But, like *Tiger Haven* and *Tara: a Tigress,* it never took off in the way that *Born Free* had a generation earlier. It could be said that Billy was unlucky in his timing: if he had come out first in the big-cat stakes, he might well have made a fortune, as Joy Adamson did. Nevertheless, in Maschler's view the book was distinguished by its author's obvious integrity, and the *London Observer* described it as containing 'invaluable material for naturalists'.

Dedicated as he now was to his animals, and a bachelor of many years' standing, Billy had by no means lost his interest in pretty girls. Women found his charm and devotion to the cause most attractive, and he was not above making a pass at any unattached young female who ventured out to Tiger Haven. Once, in London, Sarah Giles introduced him to Koo Stark, the American model whose later association with Prince Andrew hit world headlines. When Billy read somewhere that Koo was about to get married, he told Sarah how sorry he was to have missed that particular boat. It was only a whimsical little joke, but it showed that old flames still flickered in him.

ELEVEN

RHINOS AND OTHERS

For a dozen years Eelie continued to be Billy's inseparable companion. Then, as she entered old age and became gradually less mobile, she preferred to remain in the precincts of Tiger Haven, rather than risk her slower reflexes in the jungle. Often she climbed the steep concrete steps to the upper verandah, where she would lie peacefully, watching the peacocks and junglefowl feeding on grain, and the chital eating cut fig leaves on the flat field in front of the house. Her nose, however, remained as sharp as ever, and whenever she detected the scent of a tiger blowing across the river, she would hurry to a vantage point and bark loud and long.

Her attitude to visitors remained studiously non-committal: anyone she knew, she would greet courteously, but she shunned strangers, and she amazed tourists by the discrimination with which she watched showings of Survival Anglia's film *The Leopard That Changed its Spots*. Whenever Harriet appeared, she would go round behind the screen as if in search of her former companion, but when the scene shifted to Sri Lanka and the leopards there, she would bark at the appearance of her natural enemies.

Her end, when it came, was mercifully swift. She was in her fourteenth year when a cancerous growth appeared on her breast, and the disease spread with dreadful speed. Billy was agonized by the way her black-rimmed eyes, though still bright as buttons, 'became tinged with unutterable pain', and although he was stricken with grief when she died, in April 1984, he was also relieved. He felt that with her passing a part of his own life had come to an end, and when he buried her, close to the remains of Juliette and Harriet, he wept beside her grave.

Three years later Jonathan Cape published *Eelie and The Big Cats*, his moving little memoir of what, to him, had been 'the ultimate dog'. Cast in the form of a letter to her, the book recapitulated the main events of her life, and her extraordinary relationships with leopards, wolves, tigers, fishing cats and men.

The year of her passing brought some heavyweight reinforcements to the wildlife of Dudhwa. In belated response to resolutions tabled by Billy a dozen years earlier, five Greater Indian One-Horned Rhinoceroses were imported from Kaziranga, in Assam, where poaching had reached unprecedented heights, fuelled by the black-market price of over 50,000 dollars for one kilogram of rhino horn.

The aim was to provide the dwindling species with a second home, but from the start the scheme hit trouble. One female died of an abortion during the airlift, and when the survivors were turned out into an enclosure at Sonaripur, another female expired from paralysis brought on by immobilization carried out to treat a minor wound. One male succumbed to injuries sustained in a fight with a rival. Thus only two of the original group remained; but after negotiations with the authorities in the Chitwan National Park, they were reinforced by four prime females sent down from Nepal in exchange for sixteen elephants.

Because the group was still very small, experts feared that inbreeding would soon render it sterile, and in an attempt to introduce new genes, the chief wildlife warden arranged for a zoo-bred female to be added to the herd. He did this against the advice of several experts, Billy included – and sure enough, the newcomer was badly gored by the original male, barely escaping with her life before being returned to Kanpur Zoo. Another female who came down on her own initiative overland from Nepal was unfortunately killed by the male, apparently out of the aggression which builds up at mating time.

Although the first calf born in the park died mysteriously – a tiger naturally being blamed – the rest of the herd bred well, and by 2003 had increased to a dozen animals.

In the autumn of 1984 Jonathan Cape published Billy's latest book, *Tiger! Tiger!*, which he dedicated to 'The Tigers of the Dudhwa National Park'. In an eloquent Foreword John Aspinall compared him favourably with George Adamson and George Schaller, and suggested that, having studied his hero the tiger for so long, Billy had 'unwittingly grown like him. The nobility of the animal has washed off on the man.'

With Blake's great poem pre-echoed in its title, the book was an impassioned plea on behalf of the species – a review of the author's work to date, an account of the maneater problem, and an update on the Tara controversy. Once again Billy travelled to London for the book's launch, and on 31 October Aspinall gave a private fund-raising dinner on his behalf in the Aspinall Curzon Club, at 20 Curzon Street in Mayfair, at which he twisted the arms of his guests so successfully that the evening raised £11,000 for the Tiger Haven Trust. In the course of the party Billy met the American film producer Cubby Broccoli – in Amar's view a revoltingly toad-like figure, smoking a huge cigar – who talked about making a tiger film, but the idea came to nothing.

In Dudhwa Billy had been hoping to acquire another elephant, but prices kept increasing so sharply that in the end he abandoned the attempt. With some of the Aspinall money he did buy a new four-wheel-drive vehicle. Yet the greatest benefit of the fund was that it enabled him to start paying immediate compensation to local people who had lost cattle or buffaloes to tigers, and thus dissuade them from retaliating against the carnivores by poisoning carcases or booby-trapping them with amateur bombs. (The official government scheme for compensating losses was impossibly slow and ineffective.)

In November 1984 Billy suffered another blow with the assassination of his most influential supporter, Indira Gandhi, who was shot by her own Sikh bodyguards. She was succeeded as prime minister by her son Rajiv, who obtained an overwhelming victory in the general election of December that year, and in February 1985 Billy wrote to him to reiterate one of his most pressing concerns:

> With the passing years I have been increasingly obsessed with the imperative necessity of a separate service to look after wildlife. The basis of this conviction is that a revenue-earning organization like the forest department cannot function in tandem with a non-profit facility. The (wildlife) organization is mainly a punishment station for unwanted personnel ... with no continuity of service, no promotional prospects, and no pecuniary incentives.

Rajiv had not inherited his mother's passionate interest in wildlife, and Billy's key recommendation remained in abeyance. Yet at the front, in and around the park, his battle for the tigers continued, and soon he was involved in another hair-raising shoot-out.

He was bitter in his condemnation of the forest department, which, in the seven years since maneating had broken out, had done nothing to lay down rules under which people might or might not enter tiger reserves. In particular, he blamed the feeble implementation of the Tiger Watch scheme, which had been mooted in 1978 but not set up until 1983, and then had been fatally weakened by internecine feuding.

The Tiger Watch staff were supposed to monitor wildlife movements and investigate any report of cattle or a man being killed; but first the team's budget was cut by the central finance department. Next, a new vehicle allotted to it was taken away. Then the chief wildlife warden, 150 miles away at his headquarters in Lucknow, arrogated overall control of the scheme to himself, even though the job was supposed to have gone to the Dudhwa park director, who at least was on the ground, and a completely inexperienced officer was placed in immediate charge.

The result was that the scheme never functioned effectively. Even when a tiger had killed and eaten the wireless operator one night outside the range headquarters at Sonaripur, and two more men had been killed in the buffer zone outside the park boundary, the director still allowed local people to collect timber and thatching material from inside the park. Billy was not in the least surprised when four more men were killed in quick succession: as he said, nature had rebelled against human intrusion into tiger habitat. The suspected maneater was often seen close to the buildings at Sonaripur, and everyone was talking about his exceptional boldness, not least the range officer, S.D. Singh, who had met the tiger while riding his motorcycle through the forest and had done a swift about-turn. Yet still no steps were taken to safeguard the forest staff as they went about their business.

In particular, no escort vehicle was provided when, at 7 p.m. one evening in April 1985, the range officer set off with a pillion passenger on his motorbike from Salukapur, a rest house on the southern boundary of the park. He never reached home, and in the morning his machine was found lying in a hole beside the road with the headlight still flickering feebly. Elephants were fetched, and a search revealed two bodies, one on either side of the road: both men had been killed by a tiger, and although the corpse of the passenger was intact, apart from gaping wounds on the nape of the neck, that of the range officer had lost the whole of one leg and half the other. For the moment the rescue party left the bodies where they were and covered them with shrouds.

As there was no one else in the park with the experience to handle the situation, messengers summoned Billy in his capacity as honorary wildlife warden, and he drove straight out to the site, taking his double-barrelled .500 express. By the time he reached the place, a large crowd had collected and obliterated most of the evidence by walking about, but he conjectured that the range officer had seen the tiger in the beam of his headlight, had tried to turn round and had fallen off into the hole on the edge of the track. It looked as though he and his companion had then panicked and run in opposite directions, and possibly shouted to each other, thus triggering the tiger's attack reflexes.

One evening a few days earlier Billy himself had driven a party of tourists along this very road, and they had come on a tiger walking down the track. The animal had seemed excessively familiar with humans, crouching to watch the vehicle from a distance of no more than ten yards, then walking past within five yards of it, and sitting in the middle of the road. From the way it kept gazing upwards – something

Tara used to do when planning her next move – Billy felt sure it was trying to work out some way of extracting one of the humans from their steel cage.

Now it was clear beyond doubt that the tiger had turned maneater, and must be destroyed before it killed anyone else. Billy therefore mounted an elephant and advanced towards the body of the range officer. A low growl confirmed that the tiger had returned to its kill and was lurking in the heavy cover. After much chivvying, it tried to slip away, and Billy took a snap shot as its striped body flashed past a gap in the grass. The tiger grunted at the shot, but kept going. After a further chase, a second shot broke its shoulder, and a third took it low in the neck, knocking it down. Yet still it was far from dead, and, with adrenalin pumping in its blood, it got up again and took refuge in another patch of grass.

Billy felt sure that, if left for a while, the tiger would die. He therefore proposed to call off the hunt for an hour or so; but at that moment up came R.L. Singh, who had been away on some errand of his own. The park director was armed only with a 12-bore shotgun, but he insisted in joining Billy on the elephant and proceeding into the grass forthwith. In its dying spasm of energy the tiger charged out, leaped at the elephant's forehead, fell back and disappeared into the cover. As the elephant lunged and wheeled away, R.L. Singh fired a shot blindly into the grass; and when the mahout brought their mount back under control, they found the tiger lying dead, with wounds from Billy's bullets in its pelvis, shoulder and neck.

The director refused to let anyone take photographs, on the grounds that the tiger had not been officially declared a maneater, and no one had been detailed to destroy it. Later, he gave an interview to a Hindi newspaper in which he claimed that even Arjan Singh, an 'accomplished hunter', had not been able to kill the animal, and that he himself, having fallen off the elephant in the skirmish, had recovered quickly to finish it off. When Billy asked him why he told such lies, he looked offended, and said he could not be responsible for the stories that journalists wrote.

The maneater of Salukapur was of average size, ten or twelve years old, with no visible abnormalities, but in poor condition. There seemed to be no physical reason why it should have taken to killing humans; and Billy could only conclude that the overlapping of the species was again to blame,

Between these hair-raising episodes he was still keeping track of Tara, frequently seeing to her when she appeared in the Neora or along its banks. When he called to her, she showed definite signs of recognition, rolling over, opening and closing her mouth, and coming closer to him – all of which he interpreted as 'the final gesture of acceptance by an animal capable of retaliation'. Once when he found her feeding on a kill, she allowed him to approach within thirty yards before she moved off, giving a Prusten. Another morning, as he sat on a low machan waiting for her to appear with her latest family of two cubs, there suddenly emerged, right underneath him, a small black dog, which stood for a moment gazing upstream. For a split second he thought that providence had sent him a replacement for Eelie: had he called out to the stranger, he might have got it – but he was too slow. The dog hurried on, lured by the scent of the tigers' kill, and a few seconds later a piercing scream told him that it 'had fulfilled its destiny as the family of tigers grabbed it.'

Tara gave birth to her third litter – a male and a female – in March 1986, and as the hot weather came on, Billy frequently watched them along the river. One day, however, he had a setback: low snarls burst into full-throated roars as Tara threatened him from across the stream and put in a short, mock-charge along a log that had fallen over the water. Realizing that he had inadvertently come between the mother and her offspring, he withdrew, and the cubs came walking over the same log bridge. Next morning, as if to make amends for her uncouth display, Tara stopped, looked back and turned about when he called her.

That September a strange male tiger appeared on the range. Because he had one toe distinctively twisted outwards on each front foot, Billy called him Splay Toes, and from the way he coexisted peacefully with Tara and her latest family for several months, he deduced that he must be one of her sons from an earlier litter. His own relationship with the animal was close, not to say reckless: if Splay Toes was on a kill, Billy would walk towards him until he moved away. Once, though, when the tiger was guarding a dead cow, it ran at him. He slid down the bank, shouted and waved his stick. The tiger retreated, then ran at him a second time, roaring, until it was within ten yards. Billy roared back – Waah! Waah! – and at the last moment Splay Toes slunk away. Later, when Billy reckoned the tiger had become dangerous, he visited one of his kills armed with a rifle, and when he passed within five yards of the crouching carnivore, he fired a warning shot to scare him off. Afterwards, he regretted the 'pusillanimity' which impelled him to make a noise, for he believed that 'like the Androcles' lion, this tiger also knew his well-wishers', and saw himself as an acquaintance who shared the same range.

Over the years Billy walked thousands of miles on his jungle patrols, checking the movements of tiger and leopards. Although he was often threatened by animals, he was never seriously attacked, and he came to believe that the big cats accepted him 'because they thought I was some kind of honorary tiger.'

It was Splay Toes who finally put paid to Abu Bakr the goat. On the night of 7 November 1987 he walked right into the shed at the end of the Tiger Haven buildings, where the goat was tethered to a cart, and grabbed him. He then dragged the body, cart and all, about twenty-five yards along the track before the wagon rolled down a slope on to him, whereupon he bolted with a roar. By the time Billy reached the scene, the goat was dead, so he tied the corpse to a eucalyptus tree for the time being; but during the night Splay Toes returned, broke the rope, and dragged the body off into some tall grass, where he ate almost all of it.

Two days later, still feeling affection for the old buffoon, Billy sent Suresh and a colleague to bring in his remains, so that he could bury them in his private cemetery: only the horns, one hoof and a piece of skin remained, but Splay Toes was still guarding them, and he sprang at the men with a roar, mauling Suresh's arm. From outside the house Billy heard the roar, and shouted back. The tiger roared again, but then abandoned his kill, and the men brought in the sorry relics of the goat, which were duly interred in Billy's private cemetery.

Splay Toes was already under dire suspicion, for earlier that year he had killed a man on the main road between Dudhwa and Pallia, and he kept attacking domestic cattle in the buffer area of the park. Having studied his movements for some weeks, Billy realized that he was in some way incapacitated, and could not kill prey animals with tough hides – and as the tiger had taken to hanging around Tiger Haven, he feared that one of his own staff might be next on the menu. He therefore decided to divert his attention by putting out a bait on the site opposite the Double-storey Machan, and when

Splay Toes killed the buffalo during the night, his secret was revealed: four bruises on the dead animal's throat showed that the tiger had lost his canines, and, being unable to kill in the normal way, had resorted to strangulation.

Next night Tara brought her latest cubs to the kill, opened the body, fed, and allowed Splay Toes to join in the repast. Watching through binoculars as the tiger ate under the red floodlight, Billy made out that he had about a third of one canine left, and concluded that he must have been injured by a home-made bomb placed in the carcass by the owner of one of the cows that he had killed.

He reported his findings to the latest park director, Mahendra Singh, and suggested that the tiger should be baited again, so that he could be immobilized, and either destroyed or sent to a zoo. Other wildlife officers came to inspect the baiting site, and on 8 December Singh wrote to Billy acknowledging all the information he had given him, and asking his advice on how to stop the tiger becoming a confirmed maneater.

So far, so good. But then suddenly the treachery and ill-will of the tiger establishment stood revealed as never before. On the evening of 16 December Mahindra Singh arrived unannounced at Tiger Haven with three assistant conservators of the forest, six policemen, armed wildlife guards and three elephants, and proceeded to smash the Double-storey Machan, which had stood for twenty-five years, on the pretext that Billy had been using it illegally for baiting tigers to show to tourists. The posse also demolished the bridge over the Neora which had been built by forest staff, and for which Billy had given a right of way through his own land. Finally they confiscated his lighting equipment and took away his stock of dead firewood, claiming that he had stolen it from the park.

The director also banned Billy from entering the park, and put up an electric fence to keep him out.

Billy afterwards wrote a dignified protest to the chief wildlife warden, R.P. Sharma – 'I feel in view of my obvious dedication to the cause of wildlife in the park, the action taken could have been done in a more amicable and less hostile manner' – but at the time he was shattered and overcome. 'How can they do this?' he said to Amar with tears in his eyes. 'What have I ever done to them?'

No matter that he had been baiting Splay Toes for valid tactical reasons, or that he had done so with the knowledge of the park director. The authorities filed two criminal cases against Billy and Balram, for illegal baiting and for stealing wood. Billy realized that if he simply offered to pay for the wood, the matter would probably be dropped; but on the baiting charge he refused to compromise, because he had done nothing illegal.

The result was that he and Balram had to keep making the tiresome, 100-mile round trip to Lakhimpur and back – for under the Indian penal code the defendants in criminal cases may not get anyone else to represent them at hearings, but must attend in person. 'This sordid affair has now been in progress for over six months,' Balram protested to the head of the World Wildlife Fund in Delhi during May 1988. 'The indignities heaped on Billy by the park authorities are countless.'

The campaign dragged on for another year, and in Billy's view it was nothing but a protracted form of harassment, which ended only when the Congress government was suspended and the governor of the U.P. took over the administration of the state. Luckily the governor was a personal friend, and gave orders that the charges should be dropped.

The reason for the harassment was not far to seek. The park staff had been making money by allowing local people to extract timber from the forest and sell it on the market, in open breach of the Indian Wildlife Act. Maddened by the disturbance which the timber-collectors were causing, and by the increase in poaching which their activities provoked, Billy had applied to the High Court for a stay order, and this stopped the illegal removal of wood; but it also annoyed the timber-collectors and sharply reduced the popularity of the chief minister of U.P., who was trying to win voters over for the forthcoming election, and he reacted furiously by taking wildlife into his own charge, removing the incumbent park director (one of the few whom Billy liked), and appointing Mahindra Singh in his place.

Splay Toes did not kill any more humans. Billy, beset by legal problems, lost touch with him, and the tiger faded from the Tiger Haven range. Yet – as Billy noted with some satisfaction – 'Nemesis stalks both ways. The chief minister died of heart failure in a foreign country, and his party lost at the hustings.'

~

With forest officials behaving as they were, it was inevitable that Project Tiger would falter. In its early days all had seemed to be going well: every year the director of every reserve reported a satisfactory increase in tiger numbers, and on paper the national population seemed to be growing well. Gradually, however, it became apparent that the increments were fictitious, and that numbers were growing at an impossible rate: the Corbett National Park, which was supposed to have reached saturation-point with a population of forty-two tigers in 1972, returned figures of sixteen per cent growth per annum, until in 1989 it was claiming a total of 112. Each director had simply stepped up his total every year without reference to what was happening on the ground. A reserve which had thirty-eight tigers one year had forty-three the next, forty-seven the next, fifty-three the next, and so on. At one point the chief wildlife warden of U.P. publicly claimed that the Dudhwa reserve contained 104 tigers – a number which the prey species in the park could not possibly sustain – when Billy reckoned that the realistic total was nearer twenty.

Any criticism from overseas – any call for a more realistic approach – incensed the authorities, who became enraged by what they saw as attempts by foreigners to interfere with an essentially Indian project. The fact that over one million pounds had been subscribed by these outside supporters in no way reduced the feeling of pique. Nevertheless, there came a point at which the relative failure of the project could not be concealed any longer. A jubilee celebration planned for 1993 turned out, as Billy put it, to be 'more in the nature of a funeral,' with the news that the tiger population of Ranthambore – once the private shooting ground of the rulers of Jaipur, and now one of the jewels in Project Tiger's crown – had plummeted from forty-four to eighteen.

Nevertheless, that same year – 1993 – there came a change of heart in Delhi, and in a flattering letter written in December, Kamal Nath, Minister for Environment and Forests, invited Billy to join the steering committee of Project Tiger:

> You have been one of the leading lights of conservation in the country, with rare dedication and commitment. Your expertise in tiger conservation, in particular, is legendary. The steering committee of Project Tiger would benefit greatly by your

sagacious advice and guidance. Therefore I would be very happy
if you would accept to be a permanent invitee of this apex body.

Billy accepted the invitation, of course. At last, it seemed, he
might have a chance to influence policy – and at first he found
the meetings of some interest. Yet soon disillusionment set in.
He found the committee 'full of babus of all kinds' – at one
session there were forty-six people present – and when in April
1994 he was summoned by telegram to a 'crisis meeting', he
was dismayed to find no agenda and no sense of urgency. His
tedious journey – a two-and-a-half hour drive to Shahjahanpur
to catch the midnight train for the six-hour trundle to Delhi –
had been a complete waste of time. He wrote letter after letter
to Nath, who took no notice, and when he called for a debate
and a vote on the question of establishing a separate wildlife
service, Nath replied that the matter had already been
extensively debated, and decided.

~

The inertia of the babus was unchanging. But great was Billy's
delight that spring when there appeared, very close to home, a
splendid-looking young male tiger with wide stripes, pale
colouring in general, a large head and rather white face – all
characteristics of Siberian stock. Billy got a clear view of this
stranger when, as he was driving towards home, he stopped by
the river to play the roar of a tiger which he had recorded
earlier. Out came a magnificent young tiger on to the bank of
the Neora, and with a surge of excitement he realized that it
must almost certainly be a descendant of Tara. She herself had
disappeared from the range two years earlier, but this looked
very much like one of her cubs, or their offspring. It was, he
reckoned, one of the most handsome tigers he had ever seen,
and he rejoiced to think that he perhaps now had living proof

with which he could refute the bureaucrats who still claimed that his attempt to augment the population of wild carnivores had failed.

First he wrote to the latest chairman of the IUCN's Specialist Cat Group, suggesting that a DNA test should be carried out to establish whether or not the good-looking newcomer carried Siberian genes. The answer was discouraging, so next he approached the chief wildlife warden of U.P. for permission to immobilize the tiger so that a blood sample could be taken. When his request was refused, he wrote to an old wildlife colleague, Hashim Tyabjee, and through him he made contact with Dr Lalji Singh, Deputy Director of the Centre for Cellular and Molecular Biology in Hyderabad. Dr Singh told him that if he could obtain hairs from the tiger in question, a DNA test would be possible; so Billy collected some hairs from a place where the tiger had rolled near the village of Basantapur – and sure enough, when these were compared with fully Siberian samples acquired from Darjeeling Zoo, back came the verdict that there was a seventy per cent certainty that the Dudhwa animal was a hybrid of Indo-Siberian origin.

To confirm the accuracy of his analysis, Dr Singh needed samples from other Dudhwa tigers, and in July 1997 Billy sent him some hairs taken from the skins of animals killed by poachers. On 23 August Singh reported: 'Out of the four samples sent by you, three share a microsatellite allele with Indian tiger and another allele with Siberian tiger.' (An allele is a form of gene arising from mutation.) Billy was disappointed that by then the handsome young tiger had moved away, and he never saw it again; but that year a tigress which was clearly also a hybrid was run over by a train and dragged along for more than a mile trapped under the cowcatcher of the engine before being cast loose (the presence of Siberian genes was again confirmed by the Hyderabad laboratory).

For him, the case was finally proven. He already knew that Tara had produced nine cubs in her four litters, but now scientific evidence confirmed that she had rejuvenated the stock of Dudhwa tigers with her particular blend of genes. The pundits, of course, were 'very disturbed' to learn that the Indian tiger was no longer 100 per cent swadeshi and one of them, having warned that the entire species could be jeopardized by crossbreeding, suggested that 'all the Dudhwa tigers should be examined so that this can be prevented'.

The fatuity of this proposal was immediately obvious to anyone who had ever worked with wildlife – it was exceedingly difficult to set eyes on even one of the park's carnivores, let alone 'examine' them all – and Billy was scathing in his contempt for those who sought to stir up the storm in the gene cup. He pointed out that the human population of India included a mixture of Chinese, African and Nordic strains, and that 'hybridization, legitimate among humans, has often resulted in perfection of face and form'. As for tigers – he contended that the five surviving sub-species all derive ultimately from the Siberian or parent race, and that it was merely the different environments into which they were dispersed over at least six million years that brought about changes in their physical make-up. Therefore, he said, it made perfect sense to breed back towards the original strain.

~

One major cause of the overall decline was poaching. Fuelled by the insatiable demand for skins and bones from China, illegal killing of tigers was rampant all over India, and Dudhwa was particularly vulnerable, for it lay right on the Nepalese border, with the frontier unguarded, and one of the smugglers' main routes was through Nepal and Tibet. There, as elsewhere, the park staff were too poorly equipped to deal with ruthless criminals, and so badly paid that they were more likely to associate with poachers, and take a cut from their earnings, than to obstruct them (pay often came through six months late). Most of the wildlife guards were armed with ancient 12-bore shotguns, and old cartridges that might or might not go off when fired, while the poachers had AK-47 automatic rifles. In any case, the park employees were crippled by the rules obtaining in U.P. Whereas in places like Kaziranga wildlife guards were empowered to shoot poachers on sight, in U.P. the guards were allowed to fire only if they themselves had already been fired at. As Billy put it savagely, 'if the poachers shot you in the gut, you can shoot back – provided you have life left.' A further discouragement was that any guard wounded had to bear his own medical expenses.

Villagers were killing tigers by every method open to them – by shooting them, blowing them up with home-made bombs, electrocuting them with live wires draped round kills, and above all by poisoning them with pesticides. A tiger which ingested poison would probably not die for three or four hours, but during that period it would wander in small circles, half-stupefied, and easy to follow. Once it was dead, it would be flayed, and the skin pegged out in the sun to dry. Not only were people retaliating against the predators, they were earning good money by doing so: a single skin could fetch up to Rs 1.5 lakh.

Because Billy had started to pay herdsmen compensation for lost cattle out of his own pocket, he began to receive information about such felonies: in January 1997, for instance, an informer told him that two tigers had been poisoned and skinned in the village of Belalkalan, but when he discovered the names of the culprits, and passed them on to the forest department, no action was taken. The only follow-up came a month later when some high grass was burnt in the rhino enclosure, revealing the skeleton of a tiger with some skin still attached. The park authority issued a statement saying that the animal was a sub-adult which had been killed in a fight provoked by sexual jealousy. Billy dismissed this as absurd, because the skeleton bore no sign of injury, and whenever a young tiger is killed by a bigger one, the skull of the victim is invariably fractured.

~

Aspinall did not visit Tiger Haven again, but he kept up his financial and moral support, writing (in 1986), 'I am a bit weak and old to come and see you now, but I am with you in spirit, as I always was.' On 17 January 1989 Billy wrote to thank him for his annual gift of £2,500:

> There are people who occur in this world who are larger than life, but appreciation comes usually when they are gone from this polluted world, and I know you do not care what you think while you are among us. But you have the unspoken prayers of the gorillas and the tigers, symbols of the lesser primates, and cats, the world over.

Billy maintained long-range contact for the rest of Aspinall's life, sending him any bits of news that he thought might be of interest. 'We have thirty elephants in residence,' he wrote in June 1992, 'including a magnificent bull, computed to be over eleven feet (at the shoulder), with fine, upcurling tusks, locally known as Palakdonta.' In 1994, after Aspinall had been to South Africa, Billy asked, 'How are the Zulus? We could use an Impi to deal with the poachers.' Then in September 1998, having learnt that Aspers was fighting cancer, he wrote: 'I was delighted to hear that you are now on the mend, and that the prayers of the animal kingdom have been answered. It is my hope that we can meet before departing for the Happy Hunting Grounds.'

~

That hope was never fulfilled, for, after a remission, Aspinall declined again, and Billy's last letter to him was dated 12 December 1998:

> Ever so many thanks for your brave and kind thoughts and wishes for the tigers of the world. Never a fervent believer in the magnanimity of the Almighty, I have heard from various sources of the suffering inflicted by a cruel fate on a philanthropic giant. I hope and pray that the malignance may soon be out of your system.

Good wishes – from men or tigers – could not save Aspers, who died in June 2000. But his benefactions to Billy did not cease with his passing, and at the time of writing (2004), they were still coming through every year. Looking back on their friendship, Billy reflected: 'John did not hate his fellow men, but hated what man had done to the world. For such a good and philanthropic man to die in agony was tragic, but he will now rest in peace in the Valhalla of tigers and gorillas, where hopefully I will join him.'

TWELVE

FIGHTING ON

In his book *The Legend of the Maneater*, published in India in 1993 (but not in London), Billy gave a sketch of his own early life and launched a vitriolic attack on the morals and attitudes of old-fashioned tiger hunters, himself included. But the main thrust of the book was an impassioned defence of his favourite animal: again and again he recounted episodes from his own immense experience to illustrate its essential nobility, and to demonstrate that tigers always steer clear of human beings if they can, rarely, if ever, killing people unless driven by some particular cause such as physical disability, lack of normal prey or overcrowding.

It was hardly surprising that several times in the text the author sounded a valedictory note, for he was already seventy-five when the book came out, and he feared that the thirty-odd years he had spent fighting for Dudhwa's animals had been largely wasted:

It is tragic for me that, at the end of my life, I have fought a battle that can only end in defeat; yet I must soldier on. If I abandon the cause, I could never live with myself. Starting as a compulsive killer, I have run the entire gamut: conscientious evaluator to conservationist, preservationist and, ultimately, crusader. I have the satisfying feeling that, in spite of eventual failure, tempered in nature's crucible I am a more civilized person than when I began.

~

Soon after writing that, he answered some questions for a newspaper article, and his replies – which for once were not shortened or distorted – illuminated several facets of his character:

Q. What is your idea of perfect happiness?
A. Being with the tiger.

Q. What is your greatest fear?
A. Being with the human multitude.

Q. Who or what has been the greatest influence in your life?
A. Jim Corbett and F.W. Champion (the forester- photographer).

Q. What do you most dislike in others?
A. Conceit.

Q. What do you most dislike in yourself?
A. Being withdrawn.

Q. What is your most precious possession?
A. My recollections of big cats.

Q. What object do you always carry?
A. A tiger's canine.

Q. What makes you most depressed?
A. The fate of future wildlife.

Q. What do you most dislike in your appearance?
A. My wizened countenance and bald head. Old age, in short.

Q. What is your favourite word?
A. I love you.

Q. What is your favourite dream?
A. A beautiful girl.

Q. What is your nightmare?
A. Extinction of wild cats.

Q. What or who is the greatest love of your life?
A. My leopardess.

Q. What is your source of sustenance?
A. To achieve the impossible.

Q. On what occasions do you lie?
A. When I think it will do some good.

Q. What is your greatest regret?
A. That my leopardess left me before her time.

Q. What brings tears to your eyes?
A. Death of animals.

Q. How do you relax?
A. By thinking beautiful thoughts.

Q. What do you envy most in others?
A. Ability.

Q. How would you like to be remembered?
A. As a champion of voiceless animals.

Q. How would you like to die?
A. Suddenly and swiftly.

He gave that interview when he was in his seventies. Yet his concern for wildlife burned as fiercely as ever. Hammering away on his ghastly old typewriter, he campaigned ceaselessly for the introduction of enlightened policies, bombarding officials with letters and bringing out – at his own expense – pamphlets called *Cry Havoc* and *Save the Tiger: The Last Ditch*. He also wrote to the prime minister, urging him to take heed of the 'overwhelming global concern' about the fate of the tiger being expressed in many countries.

One of the most pressing needs, in his view, was to refresh the gene-pools of India's twenty-three separate tiger reserves; and since it was physically impossible to link them all together with forest corridors, along which animals might migrate, he suggested that 'chemical corridors' should be established – that tigers should be darted and translocated into different areas. Such movement would obviate the danger of inbreeding, but – as he admitted – it might also give rise to territorial disputes: the sudden arrival of a strange tiger on the patch of an established male could lead to fatal clashes. This had already happened in the Sunderbans delta, where a tiger shifted as an experiment was killed after two or three days by the resident male.

The tigers of Dudhwa were breeding as well as, if not better than, those of any other reserve, with a relatively high proportion of females and cubs to males. This he attributed to the fact that Tara had infused new vitality into the closed community, and he believed that similar reinvigoration could be achieved elsewhere, given intelligent human intervention. This, however, was one of the many proposals that the officials of Project Tiger refused to contemplate, not accepting that, without it, extinction through inbreeding would become inevitable.

The problems caused by the relentless increase in the human population were vividly demonstrated by a violent encounter that took place at Dudhwa in 1997. Suddenly about a thousand squatters came walking across country from the east: they went into the forest, hoisted a flag, started building huts and felling trees. When park officials confronted them and tried to pull down the flag, they opened fire with primitive weapons loaded with pellets, and one of the foresters collapsed. The wildlife guards then fired back, killing two people and setting off a stampede.

As Billy said, 'you couldn't really blame the squatters, because someone had given them a document saying that land was available in Kheri, and that they could go and claim it. But at the same time, you must sympathize with the animals, who have no advocate.' Characteristically, the forest department would not pay for the wounded man to receive medical assistance; but Nicky Marx, who heard about the incident, sent money for him to be treated in hospital at Lakhimpur, and Billy afterwards made up the shortfall. The man survived, but to this day has pellets embedded in his body.

Poaching continued to be a major threat – and the difficulty of trying to contain it was illustrated by an incident that took place at Tiger Haven in February 2001. In the middle of the day a white van approached the farm at speed and slid to a halt in a cloud of dust in front of the buildings. From it poured nearly a dozen men, one armed with an AK-47 rifle, another with a sub-machine gun, escorting two prisoners whom they had just captured in the forest. In command of the posse was a banker from Lucknow – let us call him X – who had become so incensed with the futility of the wildlife guards and their lamentable record in the park that he had set himself up as a freelance detective and policeman.

For the past six weeks, without the sanction or even the knowledge of the park authorities, he had been planning an elaborate sting operation, posing as a dealer who wanted to buy tiger skins and bones for export to China. After numerous meetings with middlemen, a rendezvous had been arranged for 7 a.m. that morning at a point inside the park, and to keep their date X and his men had driven out from Lucknow at two o'clock in the morning.

Dawn found them at the rendezvous, deep in the jungle, equipped not only with firearms, but also with suitcases full of counterfeit rupee notes. Three of the poachers emerged from the undergrowth to meet them, but when they suggested that X accompany them further into the trees, to show him their goods, he declined absolutely to leave the dirt road, because he knew that the gang would be armed with home-made blunderbusses, loaded with bolts and lumps of iron railing, which they would not hesitate to use.

After some negotiation, during which the fake rupees were prominently displayed, the poachers brought out one hessian sack which contained a complete tiger skin, and another full of clean, dry tiger bones. Then, in a flash, before any money changed hands, the rest of X's team erupted from the back of the vehicle, grabbed the two poachers and their sacks, and hauled them aboard.

At Tiger Haven the captives were confined in a storehouse, with an armed guard sitting outside the door. X, who knew Billy well, asked if he might leave them on the premises overnight: he did not want to hand them over to the authorities for the time being, because he had a second sting operation lined up for first light the next morning, and he knew that if he went to park headquarters, word of the first seizure would certainly get out, and the second would be jeopardized. So Billy agreed to house the prisoners overnight, and during the afternoon X drove off, leaving one of his armed men and a couple of others to act as guards, with orders to shoot the prisoners in the legs if they tried to make a break for it.

Incredible as it seems, during the early hours of the morning they did just that, escaping and running off into the forest. Even Billy could not make out how they had managed it: he could only assume that they must have promised large sums to the man on guard at the door. In any case, they vanished, and when X returned soon after first light, the second operation having failed, he was left with nothing but the skin and bones.

The skin was that of a big male tiger, with paws attached, and the fact that it was still stinking – not having fully dried out – indicated that it was only a few weeks old. The absence of bullet holes and marks made by snares or traps showed that the animal had been poisoned. The other sack contained about 70 lbs of bones – the remains of three tigers – and would have fetched fortunes if it had reached China. Billy of course was chagrined by the knowledge that the park had lost at least three more tigers, and deeply frustrated that a courageous initiative had been aborted. X, also, was keenly disappointed, for he had taken time off from work, and lost some salary.

~

In 2000 R.L. Singh had surfaced yet again to stir up trouble. By then he had become chief wildlife warden of U.P., and he sought to settle a few old scores by publishing his book *Tara the Cocktail Tigress*. Had this mendacious trash been written by a hack journalist, its inaccuracy and mediocrity might not have been so surprising; as it was, it seemed scarcely possible that a man who had held senior positions in the forest service could publish such a farrago of lies. The kindest course is perhaps to believe that, by then, the author had become a fantasist – someone who has told the same falsehoods so many times that he no longer thinks of them as inventions, but believes them to be genuine.

He published the book first in Hindi, which he knew Billy would not be able to read, and only when an English version appeared was its amazing disregard for truth exposed to a wider audience. The text contained so many obvious errors that it was hard to tell which were accidental and which deliberate. Out came the author's familiar spiel about how many people Tara had killed in the period during which he had 'the rare opportunity of protecting the Indian tiger'. In the early 1980s, he wrote:

> A series of maneating incidents made life hell for us for years to come. We began scouting for the British tigress, as she kept giving us the slip, eating one man after another. We finally caught up with the maneating tigress after she had dragged twenty-two people to their graves. And a lot of secrets came out into the open. Or should we say, her death let the cat out of the bag.

Not content with trying to warm up these old chestnuts, he launched a still more fantastical claim – that Indian tigers had become 'the target of an international conspiracy of unimaginable proportions', and that the conspirators' chosen tool was Tara, 'a cocktail tigress, airlifted from a British zoo, set free in the forests of Dudhwa National Park to dillute (sic) the purity of the Indian tiger'.

Billy could not condone such outright mendacity, and on 1 March 2000 he wrote R.L. Singh a sharp letter refuting his main points, recalling that most of the convicted maneaters had been males, reminding him that he personally had prevented any attempt to radio-collar Tara, and ending with a challenge:

You have in your possession the mounted skin of the maneater you have claimed to be Tara. As I have already suggested, a DNA test to establish (whether it contains) a Siberian strain could prove conclusive. But maybe in the words of the Earl of Montrose,

He either fears his fate too much
            Or his deserts are small,
That puts it not unto the touch,
            To win or lose it all.

I await your reply.

                              Yours sincerely, Arjan Singh

Needless to say, answer came there none.

THIRTEEN

LOOKING AHEAD

A dozen years after he told a newspaper reporter that he would like to die 'suddenly and swiftly', Billy is still battling away. In his late eighties he has inevitably slowed down: arthritis in the knees has reduced his mobility, and in any case, with no animals to train or exercise, he spends less time prowling the jungle, more at home. Nevertheless, he still gets up at dawn, even on cold winter mornings, and sits at a table on the open verandah, wearing a red woolly hat and pecking away with one finger at his trusty typewriter as he fires off pamphlets and letters at the babus, demanding the separation of forestry and wildlife management into different government organizations, and castigating Westerners for not supporting his struggle. 'The trouble with you people in the West is that you say "Save the Tiger, by all means, but save him in your own country".' Echoes of his feudal background ring out as he summons his retainers: 'Eh! Sri Ram!' he shouts. 'Eh! Boltu! Eh! Haploo!' Within seconds one or other appears with a quiet 'Ji, Sahib?', ready to find his reading glasses, tie his bootlaces or bring him a newspaper.

His latest project is to dredge the stretch of the Neora river that runs past Sathiana and his own territory, in an attempt to minimize the monsoon floods which have carpeted the grasslands with silt. Over thousands of acres inside and outside the park, the annual deposits carried down by the river out of the Nepalese hills have coarsened the vegetation to such an extent that it is no longer palatable to ungulates: this means that the area supports fewer deer, and therefore is less attractive to tigers.

The aim of the dredging is to bring the Neora back under control, but the task is by no means a simple one, for access to the river bank is difficult in many places, and the channel is obstructed by hundreds of fallen trees. Nevertheless, with financial help from the Bajaj sugar-processing factory in Pallia, a good start had been made by the end of 2004, and long stretches of the channel from the railway bridge in the east, as far upstream as Tiger Haven to the west, had been cleared. (The sugar factory's interest was sparked by the fact that the silt has started to ruin the land on which cane was being grown.)

The next step is to eliminate the coarse grasses by smashing them down or cutting them, and to replace them with sweeter species, thus helping deer to breed and encouraging the major predators to hunt in relatively safe surroundings. Experiments with various types of grass have shown that local strains are best suited to the environment.

In 2002 Billy's nephew Simon Commander, together with two of his most staunch supporters, Donald and Lucy Peck, based in Delhi, formed the Tiger Haven Society, a charitable trust designed to carry on his work when he is gone; and in 2003 Gyan Mishra, a senior wildlife officer who had recently retired from the forest service, was retained to work for the trust part-time. The hope is that Tiger Haven will continue indefinitely as a wildlife sanctuary and research station, perpetuating Billy's name. The Bombay Natural History Society has shown keen interest in the project, but so far has not had the resources to back it.

Meanwhile, the old honorary tiger, undaunted by countless rebuffs, continues to hammer away at his key contention – that commercial forestry and wildlife conservation must be run by separate government departments. 'These are the days of the specialist, when the orthopaedic surgeons, the neurologists and the cardiologists have their particular disciplines,' he wrote in a letter to Ravi Singh, Secretary General and Chief Executive Officer of the World Wildlife Fund in India, in August 2004. 'Yet wildlife is in the charge of the "general practitioner", who previously dealt with ailments from vertigo to in-growing toenails.'

Billy's letter recalled how Jim Corbett, on his way to retirement in Africa in 1947, had predicted that tigers would last from ten to twenty years. 'We are now in the twenty-first century,' Billy told Ravi Singh, 'and the tiger still has a tenuous hold on existence, though in latter years the pace of attrition has accelerated alarmingly. "Save the Tiger" is a paradoxical slogan for the preservation of magnificence – but no one wants him. The West says "Save the tiger, but save him in your own country." His neighbours hate him for his destructive potential, and seek his elimination. Due to genetic depression, fragmentation of habitat, operation of forest mafias and poaching, the tiger's future is entirely insecure.'

History will judge the success or failure of Billy's own efforts to save the species. Some big cat experts still maintain that it was folly to release a zoo-born tigress into the jungle, and claim that such artificial replenishment of wild stocks has no place in true conservation. Others believe that Billy set a magnificent example of what could be achieved. In the words of the leading American specialist Chuck McDougal, 'for dedication and single-mindedness he is in a class of his own' – a verdict echoed by that other outstanding naturalist George Schaller: 'I have tremendous admiration for him, and for what he has accomplished on behalf of wildlife.'

In December 2003, *Sanctuary Asia* magazine accorded him its Lifetime Achievement Award, calling him 'a living legend, considered by some to be the godfather of the movement to save the Indian tiger'. The magazine rightly described him as 'a thorn in the flesh of the Uttar Pradesh Forest Department', and concluded that 'he would like simply to be remembered as Arjan Singh, a man who loved tigers and fought to protect them from humans'.

In December 2004 his family, friends and supporters were overjoyed when they heard that he had won a still more important honour – the annual J. Paul Getty Wildlife Conservation Prize, administered by the World Wildlife Fund, which recognizes outstanding contributions to international conservation, and carries an award of $100,000. Sharing the prize with one other, Billy received a cheque for $50,000, and the citation saluted the 'passion and tireless devotion' which he had given to tiger preservation. Within a week he heard that Mulayam Singh Yadav, Chief Minister of UP, had conferred on him the Yash Bharati award – a glorious double culmination – the crowning moment of his career.

The Getty award was presented to him on 4 February 2005 in a moving ceremony held one evening at the headquarters of the Dudhwa National Park. More than 150 people crowded into the interpretation centre, with the park rangers in their dark olive uniforms thronging the open doorways, some with rifles slung on their shoulders.

In an affectionate speech from the dais, Ravi Singh described Billy as a latter-day Jim Corbett, and praised the unparalleled dedication with which he has fought his marathon 'battle for Dudhwa'. He spoke mostly in English, but occasionally slid into Hindi, sometimes in the middle of a sentence. Billy replied in Hindi, and other dignitaries were invited to have their say. Ripples of applause kept running through the audience, and palpable surges of emotion swept the hall as speakers sang the honorary tiger's praises.

Afterwards, the company repaired for supper to a pale mauve marquee, from which the caterers had had to evict a young hog deer before they set out their wares. Log fires blazed among the scattered trees, and all around the jungle stood silent. What if a real tiger had called out of the forest? One deep *a-oom!* would have made everyone's hair stand on end. But in the event the animals remained silent, and it was left to the humans to honour their local hero.

Even in India, where he has his critics, nobody doubts his dedication to the cause of the supreme predator. 'He was a vital player in the '70s and '80s, when Indira Gandhi was at the helm,' says the latter-day expert Valmik Thapar. 'If she had given him the wildlife service he called for – what a tremendous difference it would have made. But in any case, Billy is unique, and I have no words to describe what I feel about him. His devotion and commitment to India's wilderness are unmatchable. He is an extraordinary man, and he will never be forgotten.'

GLOSSARY

Asian elephant
Elephas maximus. More compact and tractable than the African elephant. Famous for its services to mankind.

Barasingha
Cervus duvauceli. Also known as swamp deer. Endangered species, now protected.

Black buck
Antelopa cervicapra. A type of antelope on the verge of extinction.

Chital
Axis axis. Strongly spotted deer.

Filwan
Elephant keeper or rider.

Fishing cat
Felis viverrina. Small, spotted cat.

Grey langur
Presbytis entellus. Long-tailed monkey.

Hog deer
Axis porcinus. Short-legged deer.

Indian mongoose
Herpestes griseus. Great killer of snakes and rats.

Indian tiger
Panthera tigris tigris. One of the seven sub-species of tiger that survive. Some 2,000 now live in India's parks and reserves.

Jackal
Canis aureus. Fox-sized predator, common in Dudhwa.

Jamun	*Eugenia jambolana.* Common deciduous tree.
Kakar	*Muntiacus muntjac.* Muntjac or barking deer.
Khair	*Acacia catechu.* Hardwood tree.
Krait	Very poisonous snake.
Lammergeier	*Gypeaetus barbatus.* Bearded vulture, with a wingspan of up to ten feet.
Leopard	*Panthera pardus.* Three sub-species of leopard survive in India, but all are now rare.
Machan	Shooting or observation platform, freestanding or built into a tree.
Mahawat (or Mahout)	Elephant driver.
Marsh crocodile	*Crocodylus palustris.* Also known as the mugger. Endangered species, protected but still poached for its skin.
Monitor lizard	*Varanus monitor.* Agile amphibian, up to five feet long.
Muntjac	See kakar.
Nilgai	*Boselaphus tragocamelus.* Large, ungainly antelope, living on open plains. Also known as blue cow.
Peacock	*Pavo cristatus.* National bird of India.
Porcupine	*Hystrix indica.* Preyed on by tigers and leopards.
Python	*Python molorus.* Large snake, up to 20 feet long and weighs up to 250 lbs.
Rhesus monkey	*Macaca mulatta.* Favourite prey of leopards.

Sal	*Shorea robusta*. Valuable hardwood tree. Grows to 150 feet.
Sambar	*Cervus unicolor*. Largest deer in India. Weighs up to 700 lbs.
Silk cotton tree	*Bombax malabarbaricum*.
Sloth bear	*Melursus ursinus*. Measures about six feet from nose to tail. Protected in India, Nepal and Sri Lanka. Nocturnal.
Smooth Indian otter	*Lutra perspicillata*. Common in Dudhwa.
Teak	*Tectona grandis*. Valuable hardwood tree with big round leaves.
Wild boar	*Sus scrofa*. Favourite prey of tiger.
Wild dog	*Cuon alpinus*. Rapacious carnivore. Hunts in packs. Alsatian-sized.
Wolf	*Canis lupus*. Partially protected in India.

SELECT BIBLIOGRAPHY

Brander, A.A. Dunbar, *Wild Animals in Central India*,
E. Arnold & Co., London, 1923.

Corbett, Jim, *Man-Eaters of Kumaon*, Oxford University
Press, London/New York, 1944.

Glasfurd, A.I.R., *Rifle and Romance in the Indian Jungle*, John
Lane the Bodely Head, London, 1905.

Grzimek, B. and M. Grzimek, *Serengeti Shall Not Die*,
Hamish Hamilton, London, 1960.

Kala, D.C., *Jim Corbett of Kumaon*, Ankur Publishing House,
New Delhi, 1979.

McDougal, Charles, *The Face of the Tiger*, Rivington Books
and Andre Deutsch, London, 1977.

Mountfort, G., *Saving the Tiger*, Studio, London, 1981.

Sankhala, K., *Tiger!*, Collins, London, 1978.

Schaller, George B., *The Deer and the Tiger*, University of
Chicago Press, Chicago, 1967.

___ *The Serengeti Lion*, University of Chicago Press,
Chicago, 1972.

Singh, Arjan, *Tiger Haven*, Macmillan, London, 1973.

___ *Tara: a Tigress*, Quartet Books, London, 1981.

___ *Prince of Cats*, Jonathan Cape, London, 1982.

___ *Tiger! Tiger!*, Jonathan Cape, London, 1984.

___ *Eelie and the Big Cats*, Jonathan Cape, London, 1987.
___ *The Legend of the Maneater*, Ravi Dayal, New Delhi, 1993.
___ *A Tiger's Story*, HarperCollins, New Delhi, 1999.
___ *Watching India's Wildlife: The Anthology of a Lifetime*, Oxford University Press, New Delhi, 2003.
Rathore, Fateh Singh, Tejbir Singh and Valmik Thapar, *With Tigers in the Wild*, Vikas Publishing House, New Delhi, 1983.